Grovelling and Other Vices

Grovelling and Other Vices

The Sociology of Sycophancy

ALPHONS SILBERMANN

Translated by Ladislaus Löb

THE ATHLONE PRESS
LONDON & NEW BRUNSWICK, NJ

First published in 2000 by
THE ATHLONE PRESS
1 Park Drive, London NW11 7SG
and New Brunswick, New Jersey

© 2000 The Athlone Press

Originally published under the title *Von der Kunst der Arschkriecherei*
Copyright © 1997 by Rowohlt. Berlin Verlag, Reinbek bei Hamburg

British Library Cataloguing in Publication Data
A catalogue record of this book is available
from the British Library

ISBN 0 485 11544 1

Library of Congress Cataloging-in-Publication Data
Silbermann, Alphons.
    [Von der Kunst der Arschkriecherei. English]
    Grovelling and other vices : the sociology of sycophancy / Alphons
Silbermann ; translated by Ladislaus Löb.
        p.   cm.
    Includes index.
    ISBN 0-485-11544-1 (cloth : alk. paper)
    1. Allegories.   2. Symbolism in art.   3. Toadyism.   4. Arts and
society.   I. Title.
NX650.A44S5513   2000
302.5'4--dc21   99-37793
                                                                      CIP

Distributed in the United States, Canada and South America by
Transaction Publishers
390 Campus Drive
Somerset, New Jersey 08873

Typeset by Columns Design Limited, Reading
Printed and bound in Great Britain by
Cambridge University Press

Blessed art Thou,
O Lord our God, King of the Universe,
who hast bestowed insight on the cock
to tell the day from the night.

From the Hebrew Morning Prayer

Contents

Contents

List of Illustrations

Illustrations

Research for illustrations by Margot Wössner. Thanks
are due to Gesina Kronenburg and Attila Erdig, Art and
Museum Library, Cologne.

I

Setting the Mood
Knigge, 'On Social Intercourse'

Setting the Mood

Once again the time had come to sort out my messy book collection. Over the years I had accumulated so many works of scholarship and literature that I often had to spend hours looking for a particular title in one of my various fields of interest – hours which, for a man of advanced age, were becoming more precious every day. And yet, being a relatively tidy person, I had arranged the shelves along the walls of my apartment, as well as I could, according to subjects. In the study three walls are full of sociology and Judaica. In the living room a wall several metres in length holds books on art and culture, with half a wall devoted to complete editions of classical authors and novelists worth keeping. The passage leading from the hall to the living room is lined on both sides with writings on music, and at the end are biographies and bibliophiles' editions of varying importance that I had found or been given.

As I had already noticed on earlier occasions, the operation of sorting, seeking and finding books according to their subject matter has the fatal disadvantage that one easily loses oneself in browsing –

stumbling over a long-forgotten possession, one feels the urge to glance again at some of the pages. The disorderly pile of volumes sent or given to me contained, among others, the first edition of the speech 'Deutschland und die Deutschen' (Germany and the Germans) that Thomas Mann – whom I regard more highly as a brilliant writer than as a human being – gave in Washington on the occasion of his seventieth birthday. According to my own system, I had to place this treasure – with its slightly arrogant refrain 'Germany is wherever I am', which recurs throughout Thomas Mann's work – on the neglected bibliophiles' shelf at the end of the passage. As I did so, I imagined myself caressing with great delight the row of foundlings which had secured a home with me over the decades, although I can by no means call myself a real collector. One of the fattest and therefore most conspicuous among them was the first edition of Adolph von Knigge's *Über den Umgang mit Menschen* (On Social Intercourse), published in 1788, which is generally regarded by Germans as the ultimate guide to etiquette.

Here my memory leaped back to my youth. How often the name of Knigge was held up by my parents as a model of good behaviour whenever I spoke with my mouth full, picked my nose, answered back, or was otherwise naughty – just as the name of Adam von Riese, the author of the earliest German textbooks on arithmetic, was held up as a model of accuracy. These names meant nothing to me, and I am inclined to believe that my parents too were only repeating common phrases from the Wilhelmine period. But now, at a time when there are so many complaints about the bad behaviour of the young, I felt I had to take this 'Knigge' to heart.

But lo and behold, as I delved into what seems a pretty turgid book to our taste, I found hardly a word about 'behaviour' in the sense in which this fairly timeless concept presents itself to us today. This was not a work of etiquette, not a manual of the *haute école* of good behaviour in respect of table manners, politeness, social graces, external appearance, abstention from swearing and cursing, and the like. I have no doubt that neither my parents nor the many others who wielded 'Knigge' like an imperious truncheon had ever read the book. They probably had no idea who this Knigge was and what he was trying to achieve with his long treatise. It is therefore necessary to stop briefly to close this gap in our knowledge, particularly since good old Knigge is still haunting the world of education as a 'book of good behaviour' worthy of quotation.

Baron Adolph Franz Friedrich Ludwig von Knigge was born on 16 October 1752 in Bredenbeck near Hanover and died at the age of 43 on 6 May 1796 in Bremen. He was of noble descent, well brought up and fairly educated, but poor. He earned his living by hiring himself out to princely families for the fair-to-middling position of chamberlain, and by writing, for very little money, about all kinds of subjects, which are of little interest to us here. The baron's lack of a steady job (as we would call it today) is demonstrated by the fact that we first find him for a while in Frankfurt, then in Heidelberg, then in Hanover and finally, till his death, in Bremen.

In the few biographies and dissertations which have been written about him – based on his four-volume autobiography *Der Roman meines Lebens* (The Novel of My Life), which began to appear in 1781 – he is referred to as a 'German aristocrat', as 'the nobleman as bourgeois', as a 'courtier' and, more pejoratively, as a 'court sycophant'. The inscription on his grave reads: 'He was the citizens' friend, a man of the enlightenment, a teacher of nations' – epithets attesting his closeness to the ideas of the 1789 French Revolution. It is known that when he began to write *Über den Umgang mit Menschen* in Hanover at the age of 36 he was suffering acutely as a result of courtly intrigues and cabals, envy and resentment, and disputes over his property.

Whether Knigge's book, bursting as it is with nobility and virtue, is labelled a work of education, a practical guide through life, or a blueprint for a humane culture – having read it from beginning to end, one recognizes everywhere the voice of an idealist marked by bitter experience. Knigge tries to improve the thoughts and actions of men in order to make life on this earth more bearable. In his search for good fortune, happiness and success, as a child of the enlightenment, he believes in the almost unlimited educability of man. He never wavers in praising this to the skies, and his precepts range from prosaic demands, like 'Keep your keys and all your other things where you can find them even in the dark', through exhortations to independence, like 'Always be completely yourself', to maxims which seem to me to suggest Kantian dimensions, like 'Be as strict with yourself as you are with others'. Such aphorisms, suggesting that a philosophy of life must be an essential feature of all intellectual attitudes, run through the whole book. However, when it comes to a *practical* philosophy of life concerned with virtues and vices, morality and immorality, purpose and utility, and when the baron, reflecting on the circumstances of his own life, raises the banner of decency and refinement, we hear a very different tune.

Thus we read right at the beginning in the introduction to the first part (quoted from the new edition of 1964) about

> what the French call *esprit de conduite* ... the art of social intercourse – an art often more readily acquired by untutored simple minds than by intelligent, wise and witty ones; the art of ensuring that one is noticed, recognized and respected, without being envied; of adjusting to the temperaments, insights and inclinations of others, without being false; of adopting with ease the tone of any society, without either losing one's individuality or stooping to base flattery.

This is all very well. Knigge is not preaching flattery or servility, but then in his next sentence he promptly invites us to acquire 'flexibility, sociability, compliance, tolerance, self-denial at the right time, control of violent passions, guardedness, and the serenity of a constantly even temper'.

What kind of attitude is hidden behind these ambiguous high principles articulated by a man who dreams of the ideals of humanity and tolerance, and who, for the sake of self-improvement and happiness, expects us to develop toughness, enlightenment, common sense, generosity, benevolence, professional efficiency, useful knowledge and skills, worldly wisdom and honesty? What is the meaning of this vacillation between reason, reality and irrationality, this message from the times of the Enlightenment and Storm and Stress? Could Knigge's pen possibly have been guided by a confessional urge when he was writing *Über den Umgang mit Menschen?* Some doubts were already voiced by Schleiermacher when he wrote in his essay 'Über die gute Lebensart' (On Good Form) that Knigge's book was only a 'Baedeker of good manners', something purely formal without substance. Certainly Knigge, with his noble demeanour, did not intend to lead us by our noses. Quite the contrary. Regardless of what he is writing about, his arguments are always devoted to moral improvement. However, in his struggle between reason and passion he fails to eschew corruption.

This corruption may be called obsequiousness, submissiveness or opportunism, sycophancy, flattery, crawling, toadying, servility, self-abasement, or indeed baseness – in the last analysis, let us say it loud and clear, it is the behavioural pattern of *grovelling* in all its facets.

I have no desire to offend Mr Knigge or those who have been roaming the pedagogical landscape for centuries carrying *Über den Umgang* with them as a glittering collection of reassuring propositions. Nor do I wish to criticise those who would attribute socio-psychological merits to Knigge by trying to perceive throughout his work penetrating insights into the nature of society and the search for an understanding of the connection between external forms and both external and internal harmony. I only want to demonstrate that no other book among all the writings on social relations expounds the usefulness, effectiveness and inveterateness of grovelling with such flexibility and such immaculate discretion. Without exaggeration, Knigge's book *Über den Umgang mit Menschen* is virtually a compendium of complaisance, a manual of grovelling.

II

Concepts

*The gentleman is kindly requested to kiss
Satan's backside*

George Bickham, Idol-worship or the way to
preferment (1740)

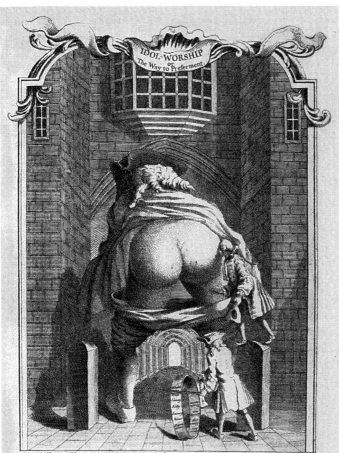

IDOL-WORSHIP
or
The Way to Preferment.

*And Henry the KING made unto himself a great IDOL, the likeness of which was not in Heaven above, nor
in the Earth beneath; and he reared up his Head unto ÿ Clouds, & extended his Arm over all ÿ Land; His Legs also
were as ÿ Posts of a Gate, or as an Arch stretched forth over ÿ Doors of all ÿ Publick Offices in ÿ Land, & whosoever went out,
or whosoever came in, passed beneath, & with Idolatrous Reverence lift up their Eyes, & kissed ÿ Cheeks of ÿ Postern.*

Chronicle of the Kings, page 31.

Concepts

🐦

I admit that I was induced to write this book by my reading of Knigge and by the desire to penetrate the veil hiding our notions of the correct or incorrect treatment of people of our own, or of a different, class. After all, I have been engaged for years in writing and speaking about the peculiarities of everyday human behaviour and its effects on our actions in society as a whole. This kind of thing is called 'the sociology of everyday life' – a term which causes many of my illustrious colleagues to turn up their noses. But I don't care. Throughout my eventful life my everyday experiences have shown me that each of us is surrounded by grovellers and that we too pay our tribute to grovelling when necessary. It is a question not of dishonesty but of prudence. And insofar as a sociologist considers it his task to devote his analysis to the well-being of society, the question of grovelling in everyday life needs to be addressed, in a spirit of enlightenment rather than moralizing, from four directions. First: how does grovelling manifest itself and how do I recognize it? Second: how do I defend myself against grovellers? Third: how do I myself grovel? Fourth: what is the purpose of grovelling?

In dealing with this topic I shall confine myself, following my own way of thinking, to the sociological aspects, rather than lose my way in the history of manners or the troublesome depths of psychological reflection. This objective demands, in the first place, a clarification of the concept of grovelling. No acute linguistic awareness is needed to realise that 'grovelling' carries a variety of meanings, depending on how and why a person behaves in a certain way or, in other words, what segment of the mentality of grovelling he is moving in. Does the groveller practice insincerity, baseness, obsequiousness or submissiveness, does he rely on enticement, defamation or compliments, and can he be accused of being a pussyfooter, a lickspittle, a scandalmonger or a toady?

This is a very wide subject, and I am certain that I have overlooked many other ingredients of the interpretation of grovelling. To ensure clarity it is necessary to devise a filter for this extremely confusing variety. To avoid misunderstanding one single word must suffice. For language is not an organism which obeys its own laws, but the expression and idiom of socially linked individuals. I have therefore decided to dispense with the affected refinement of Knigge, and to adopt a coarse word which comprises many different forms of grovelling. The word, in German, is *Arschkriecherei*, literally 'arsehole-crawling', which is best translated into English as arse-licking. O dear, people will say, such a vulgar word in the mouth of an educated man! But usage is after all the highest proof of linguistic accuracy and of the unvarnished truth, to which I have always been committed.

Furthermore, this uncouth word encompasses both symbol and gesture. It implies more than the definition 'a person given to excessive flattery', suggested by *Duden*, the omniscient arbiter of German usage, or 'groveller, obnoxious flatterer', as the authoritative *Deutsches Wörterbuch* states tersely. To come to terms with reality, a sociological reflection must focus on a social fact, even if this 'only' appears in a banal, everyday shape. Distinctions of meaning and expression must be brought to a central point, which should have as much symbolic force as possible. Bottom, posterior, derriere, as the more polite allusions to this part of the anatomy run, have become a concrete graphic sign to express abstract ideas or feelings, and so has the arse (by courtesy of Goethe's hero Götz von Berlichingen, who invites an enemy to 'lick my arse'). Whether it is a kick in the arse or the erotic wiggle of the fashion model's arse, our consciousness, labouring under an insatiable desire to make distinctions, substitutes the symbol for the reality: the reality is perceived via the symbol.

Gestures – seen either as the totality of expressive body movements, or individually as a movement of the arm, the hand, the lips or the head – are at one and the same time attitudes, signs, symbols and actions expressing states of mind. For example kneeling, depending on the occasion, may be a sign of reverence and respect or of servility and self-abasement, but also a sign of deception and pretence. When it comes to arse-licking – or 'You can kiss my arse', as the English also put it without beating about the bush – symbol and gesture merge into a whole, in which the one hides the other.

To avoid embarrassment in investigating a matter which is repulsive to many people, I looked for support in generally respected works of literature. I remembered performances of Goethe's *Faust*, in which Mephistopheles, followed by his retinue, always appeared with a bare bottom in the Walpurgis Night scenes of both the first and the second part of the drama. I consulted my edition of Goethe, but to my surprise was unable to find either a stage direction or a reference in the text to that effect. Could it be that prudish editors or adaptors have cut our weighty classic?

It was as if fate had intervened when I came across Albrecht Schöne's undistorted edition of Goethe's *Faust*. The admirably meticulous editor supplies not only an authentic text but also includes many passages from Goethe's drafts, which Goethe himself – who was obviously never at a loss for a pithy word – dropped from the final version of the monumental work. The passage referring in terms of both symbol and gesture to Mephistopheles's bare bottom, which now regularly appears in performances – and with it the intepretation of arse-licking, or 'arse-crawling' as the German language has it – reads in Schöne's stage version as follows:

(KNIENDER
... und kann ich, wie ich bat,
Mich unumschränkt in diesem Reiche schauen,
So küss ich, bin ich gleich von Haus aus
Demokrat,
Dir doch, Tyrann, voll Dankbarkeit die Klauen.
(*Mephisto als*) ZEREMONIENMEISTER
Die Klauen! Das ist für einmal!
Du wirst dich weiter noch entschließen müssen.
(KNIENDER)
Was fordert denn das Ritual?
ZEREMONIENMEISTER
Beliebt dem Herrn, den hintern Teil zu küssen!
(KNIENDER)
Darüber bin ich unverworrn,
Ich küsse hinten oder vorn.
              (*Satan wendet sich*)
Scheint oben deine Nase doch
Durch alle Welten vorzudringen,
So seh ich unten hier ein Loch,
Das Universum zu verschlingen.
Was duftets aus dem kolossalen Mund!
So wohl kanns nicht im Paradiese riechen,
Und dieser wohlgebaute Schlund
Erregt den Wunsch hineinzukriechen.
(*Atemlose Stille. Dann frenetischer Aufschrei der Menge*)
Was soll ich mehr?
SATAN (*richtet sich auf, wendet sich um*)
              Vasall, du bist erprobt!

Hierdurch beleih ich dich mit Millionen Seelen.
Und wer des Teufels Arsch so gut wie du gelobt,
Dem soll es nie an Schmeichelphrasen fehlen.

[Prose translation:
  (KNEELING MAN)
  ... and, tyrant, if I may look around freely in this
  realm as I asked, I will kiss your claws in grati-
  tude, though I was born a democrat.
  (Mephisto as) MASTER OF CEREMONIES
  The claws will do for a start. But thou'lt have to
  do more than that.
  (KNEELING MAN)
  What does the ritual demand?
  MASTER OF CEREMONIES
  The gentleman is kindly requested to kiss Satan's
  backside.
  (KNEELING MAN)
  That doesn't confound me. I can kiss back or
  front.
  (Satan turns round)
  While your nose above seems to penetrate all the
  worlds, down here I see a hole to swallow the
  universe. What odour comes from this colossal
  mouth! There can't be so good a smell in
  Paradise, and this well-built abyss arouses the
  desire to crawl into it.
  (Breathless silence. Then a frantic outcry from
  the crowd)
  What more shall I do?

SATAN (straightens himself, turns round)
Vassal, thou hast passed the test! Hereby I enfe-
off thee with millions of souls. And having
praised the devil's arse so well, thou shalt never
want for terms of flattery.]

III

Virtue and Vice
Human, All-too-Human

Paul Klee: Meeting of two men believing each other to hold a higher position (1903)

Virtue and Vice

In whatever form and context arse-licking manifests itself, be it in private or public life, it is commonly regarded as immorality or vice. Even when it is used to conceal deficiencies, to achieve agreement, adjustment and adaptation, or to replace a sense of inferiority with a sense of superiority - it is still seen as a lack of values, or indeed virtues. But is this really true? Is the phrase 'making a virtue of necessity' only a futile plea for pity and understanding?

Here, as a sociologist studying the behaviour of people in society, I am assailed by doubts. I must not allow myself to be pushed into either idealisation or defamation in my search for knowledge. What does virtue mean today? Is it still thought about and, if so, what is actually regarded as virtue or vice? If anything at all, virtue is said to signify a sense of duty, respect, obedience or fidelity; in Platonic terms, wisdom, moderation, courage and justice; or cheerfulness as opposed to melancholy, admiration as opposed to contempt - and all this is placed in the ethical or moral keeping of a steadfast disposition, or alternatively treated as acquired, morally valuable, qualities.

Without elevating arse-licking to a virtue, we must ask whether it is really enough to assign any kind of virtue to the realm of doing good. After all, virtue essentially depends on two factors, namely the custom of doing good and the strength of the soul or, in more imaginable terms, strength of character. Consequently I believe that an honest action carried out from time to time is not sufficient to constitute virtue. Even an act of sublime devotion, if it is not merely the result of earlier habits, is inspired by instinct or momentary excitement. Moreover, the quality of virtue is due not only to an innate inclination towards goodness, but also to the effort needed to apply and exercise it. However lucky those who have virtuous qualities may count themselves, it is not possible to rule out either weakness or serious mistakes, since those qualities derive from disposition and character and not only from the will. How often do circumstances and opportunities drive us to arse-licking, simply because we lack the strength and courage to resist it?

Both virtue and vice set themselves a goal and are determined by the motives underlying them, that is, they are activated by factors which lie outside the good or bad that they are trying to achieve. Without going into the subtleties of moral philosophy, everyday virtues and vices require two incentives: the hopeful expectation of reward, thanks or happiness, and the fear of grief or punishment. While rewards bring satisfaction, punishments give rise to remorse, not to mention any other sensations that accompany one or the other. Certainly, virtue and vice are not the same thing to all people. They differ according to age, sex, occupation, education and other characteristics, so that we have to agree that some virtues may be attributed to some people but not to others – and may indeed even become vices. Is the virtue of goodness not often a sign of weakness?

Now I would dearly love to tackle what I have identified as arse-licking in its everyday form from the angle of virtue and vice. I could wave the torch of the passionate moralist, and find myself shunted into the sidings of defence mechanisms such as regression, identification, compensation or sublimation. However, by doing so I would be handicapping my task from the beginning, instead of approaching a delicate, and for all that no less human, phenomenon objectively and factually. As a sociologist concerned with society, culture and human self-conception, I know that values need to be regarded as facts, and facts as values. As it is not like me to practice pseudo-sociology consisting of empty generalizations, cheap truisms and speculative follies, I cannot avoid describing and comprehending the human, all-too-human phenomenon of arse-licking in proven sociological terms.

If one does not wish to devalue either the conceptual sign or the notional content of arse-licking by flaunting it as a blunt and thoughtless banality, obscenity or profanity, then one must move it, with or without censure, out of its material environment and regard it as a *manifestation of life*. One must integrate it objectively into social relationships, where the individual relates his own actions, feelings and thoughts to those of others like him. Whether one has man's sociable or social nature in mind, interpersonal relationships are part of the human make-up. The individual knows that most of his actions, including arse-licking with all its hidden causes, affect others, and that those others will respond with actions which will interfere with his own existence. In acknowledgement of this fact sociology has developed the central and fundamental concept of 'interaction', or the reciprocal relationship between actions. Without going into the subtleties of interactionism, the manifestation under study can be regarded as interaction. It results either in cohesion, unanimity and solidarity, or in opposition, contradiction, hostility and antagonism, or in a mixture of both.

If we consider arse-licking in this light – as something situated within the framework of interaction – we arrive by a straight route at an understanding of human *behaviour*, that is, of human actions, be they latent or manifest, overt or covert. And since such actions always involve others, arse-licking must be regarded as a social action. Given that social actions of this kind occur in all social classes and constantly repeat themselves, they become customs, just as individual actions, repeated often enough, become habits. Customs are social habits, which have become the foundations of social behaviour through repetition.

In delimiting our topic in sociological terms we

must explain that 'customs' can have different names, according to whether what is to be highlighted is their character or the situation in which they are followed. Let us consider some of them. 'Conventions' signify common agreement concerning customs. 'Traditions' are customs of long standing. 'Rituals' are customs with symbolic meanings. 'Ceremonies' are customs marking important events. The terms 'etiquette' and 'propriety' are used for certain customs in 'high society' and protocol. And finally 'manners', which exercised old Knigge so greatly, are customs which are assumed to be founded on consideration for other people in social life.

All these labels refer to expectations which create a stable connection between good conduct and well-being. It is only when these expectations prove to have been violated or disgraced – as they do in the case of arse-licking – that one speaks of deviant behaviour. Only in such cases does the individual pay himself in the counterfeit currency of his dreams.

I do not wish to fill pages weaving the present topic into the fabric of sociology, for example by relating it to norms, roles or structures. But if I am to interpret social reality adequately with the help of sociology I must not overlook the essential connection between arse-licking and *social control*. First I must note that in the social sciences the term 'social control' has many different layers of meaning and describes a number of different facts. In its simplest form it means that the action of one person predetermines the reaction of another. Control is exercised positively through material or symbolic rewards, negatively through coercion or punishment. The aim of bringing about a prescribed or expected action may require domination – domination of one person over another person, of a group over its members, of a group over another group, or of the representatives of a state over all the groups in a certain society. The method of control may be formal or informal.

Arse-licking may well be such an informal method of control. For instance, the freedom of the individual may be infringed by the insinuations of gossip. How does that work? First, gossip will serve as a method of social control for the tale-bearer, who is expressing disapproval of the deviant behaviour of the object of his tales ('Your honour is at stake, people say your wife is deceiving you'). Further, gossip will exercise social control over its victim by pressurizing him into changing his behaviour according to the expectations of his environment, and in particular those of the inane arse-licker. Finally, gossip wrapped in flattery will become a method of social control by producing conformity preventively, like a threat. The consequences that such gossip can have as a method of social control – for example, murder – were demonstrated centuries ago by Shakespeare in his play *Othello*.

IV

Purposive Ideology
Neither good nor evil

Johann Michael Voltz: The new King of the Universe (1814)

Der neue Universalmonarch
auf dem, zum Wohl der Menschheit errichteten Throne.

Our sociological consideration of arse-licking so far has produced a rather negative, selfish image of man, as a hurtful phrase like 'this character is an arse-licker' demonstrates. In view of such negative connotations it would seem reasonable to be lenient, try to make excuses and even look for examples bordering on altruism. But this would be tantamount to regarding sociological reflection as a pernicious luxury rather than an indispensable addition to our way of living.

Is it not also necessary to know about the consequences of arse-licking whether these be dubious or harmless? Let us therefore attempt to outline them in terms of the phenomenon itself. We could talk about rewards – meaning recognition or specific returns, material or symbolic, benefiting the arse-licker. We could talk about punishments – meaning pain, suffering or grief incurred as a result of performing or not performing an act of arse-licking. We could refer to agreement in the sense of conforming to customs in our attitudes or actions, and to disagreement, meaning either our failure to conform to customs or indeed opposition to them by our attitudes or actions. Finally we could mention our awareness of the threat of social injury, that is, thinking or feeling that we shall be punished because of our disagreement.

All this seems to me a very clumsy attempt at identifying socially conditioned patterns of behaviour behind the detrimental or profitable everyday effects of arse-licking. Our friend Knigge adopted a much simpler approach. To avoid trouble between people, he simply warned us not to put our inner worth – 'which will always remain gold, even when hidden like a treasure under the earth' – at risk. Although he did not say what this 'inner worth' was supposed to be, we should not ignore his highly poetic statement. After all, arse-licking does comprise some values which we ought to make it our concern to appreciate.

Let us do it the easy way, without a lot of profound psychologizing, by noting that the value of arse-licking in everyday life is determined by desire, need and interest understood as sympathy, advantage, profit or pleasure. The pursuit of our complex desires, needs and interests may extend to values equipped with techniques of arse-licking. The strength – or range of influence – of these values depends chiefly on their validity.

Seen from a rather idealistic angle, as for instance in Knigge, three fundamental values stand out in our society, to which all other values, including arse-licking, are attached: the good, the beautiful, the true. According to the Greek philosophers it is from these values that ethics, aesthetics and logic, with their respective forms of judgement, derive. However, as social philosophers have demonstrated, this ignores the fact that there is not only one ethic and one logic running through society, but that these things have many different sides. By saying that this or that instance of arse-licking is good I am separating it from one which is bad or even evil. But what seems good or bad to one person does not necessarily do so to another. The fact is that value judgments vary considerably. In elucidating what is simply described as arse-licking we must therefore be clear that the act itself – ranging from dissembling to adaptation – cannot *be* good or evil but is only evaluated as one or the other. Ultimately it is the members of society who attribute the negative quality of being 'bad' to the kind of conduct which they despise, and the positive quality of being 'good' to that which they regard as commendable.

The differences in values and value judgments have led to the liberating statement that 'the end justifies the means'. As so often, this statement too has become a proverb which ignores the consequences. For the means often have quite unexpected consequences, which are very different from the ends being consciously pursued. In discussing our topic we must therefore make a clear distinction between the value of the means and the value of the ends, which ultimately signifies that the ends never justify the means.

It takes no particular penetration to realise that the value of the various acts of arse-licking is determined by their purpose and usefulness – which sets in motion a part socio-psychological, part ideological process ending in a positive or negative outlook. If by ideology we mean a totality of related ideas, concepts, judgments, conclusions, evaluations and hypotheses, and not merely the defence system of an individual or a group, then we are bound to realise that arse-licking is a *purposive ideology*. In other words, it is a complex of ontological statements, value judgments and insinuations which do not serve the search for the truth or the appropriate analysis of the connections between things, but which are designed to *justify the behaviour* of the individual or the group, whether by concealment or by deception.

The pragmatic elements in arse-licking, seen in my terms as a purposive ideology, are so substantial that they can easily be unmasked by being confronted with rational insight. This will be the topic of the chapters which follow.

V

Opportunism

When to submit

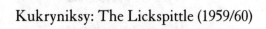
Kukryniksy: The Lickspittle (1959/60)

Opportunism

I shall probably be accused of having chosen a basically detestable or indeed disgusting topic. But this is
what happens when a sociologist contemplates everyday life instead of posing as a starry-eyed idealist bent
on improving the world or society – which of course
carries no particular obligations. I do not intend to set
the cat among the pigeons but rather to demonstrate,
taking account of times and customs, both the dark
and the light sides of a type of human behaviour
which is purposively geared to success.

It is not a mind-blowing insight that our actions –
including arse-licking in thought and deed – are
determined on the one hand by our individual relationship to certain values and on the other by the like-
lihood of our reaching a goal. Whether reaching a
goal which involves values is regarded as success or
failure differs from one person or group to another,
and it is therefore not possible to generalize. Whether
one humbly takes 'the road to Canossa', cynically
declares 'Paris well worth a Mass', or fatalistically
claims that 'nothing will come of nothing' and 'God
helps those who help themselves' – a certain purpose
is guaranteed to be served in each case.

This alone would be sufficient reason for the impossibility of attaching the ancient phenomenon, which I am in the process of clarifying in relation to the whole of society, to any particular literary characters who could be classified as arse-lickers, for example Shakespeare's courtiers Rosencrantz and Guildenstern. It is even less appropriate, in my view, to turn oneself into some kind of informer exposing temporary or permanent arse-licking in specific personalities, dead or alive. Moreover, I am reluctant to abandon the sensibility demanded from a sociologist, particularly in connection with a topic that many people find annoying. What, then, is to be done? Should I invoke the worldly wisdom of behavioural guidelines to happiness, such as prudence or honesty, lust for fame or power, arrogance, pettiness or mistrust? All this, however, would set me on the wrong track – on the one hand because our competitive culture includes certain methods of arse-licking which the members of our society are taught from the earliest age, and on the other hand because people's social goals and desires unfold in the immediacy of a social framework, that is, in an environment of spontaneous and unavoidable interpersonal partnerships.

Consequently I cannot put my hand in my pocket and pull out adjectives such as practical, conciliatory, conservative, public-spirited, successful, etc. to bestow on arse-licking as practised by one or other well-known public personality. If I am not prepared to forswear Pascal's dictum that 'thought constitutes the greatness of man' – if, in other words, I believe that man is guided by reason in spite of all his confusion – then I must track down arse-licking not merely as a pattern of behaviour dictated by a purposive ideology but as a mode of social intercourse within an existing system of communication. But that is only possible if interpersonal communication is projected onto a meaningful plane satisfying the requirements of a typology. I will therefore sift through the thicket of arse-licking according to its different types, which is the only enlightened way in which we can do it justice and avoid becoming useless moralizers.

The sociological exploration of everyday events and actions – that is, the sociology of everyday life – must be situated between apprehension and assurance. In specifying the different types of arse-licking, therefore, it is necessary to separate, for example, ruse and stratagem from force and coercion, disregard and contempt from abuse and insult. The assessment of arse-licking at an everyday level disregards these distinctions. If one asks what is implied, the first answer usually refers not to morality or vice, treachery or impropriety, but to *opportunism*, of a subtle or clumsy kind: the behaviour of the arse-licker is said to have been opportune, i.e. convenient, appropriate or useful.

Such assertions accept arse-licking in a liberal manner, without either restraining or condemning it, even though opportunism contradicts the idea of following convictions. This emerges clearly from the many

definitions – short or long – of 'opportunism' in dictionaries. I like the following comprehensive one best:
opportunism consists not so much in behaving in
accordance with moral principles or a concerted plan,
but rather in using the circumstances of the moment
to serve one's own interests to one's greatest advantage. In this, as in other definitions, advantages gained
through actions are always in the foreground. In plain
language, any act of arse-licking which is motivated
by, and identifiable with, opportunism aims to have an
effect, be that either beneficial or harmful.

This statement, with its moral echoes, could lead us
into the trap of philosophical value judgements of the
kind underlying, for example, utilitarianism, that is,
the school of thought which regards the benefit accru-
ing to the individual or to the community as the purpose of all human actions: if an action produces an
excess of useful effects over detrimental ones it is
right, otherwise it is wrong.

The emphasis in such an evaluative way of thinking
rests on the consequences of actions, regarded as right
or wrong, and not on the motives. But it is precisely
the motives that we seek if we consider opportunism
as one of the forms of arse-licking in action. To some
people utilitarianism as an ethical theory may be close
to opportunism, but to equate the two, as is often
done, or simply to confuse them in linguistic usage, is
fundamentally flawed.

As soon as opportunism is discussed as an entity
removed from the fulness of life it tends to be

regarded as a human proclivity based on common sense. We are told in abstract terms that opportunism is an intellectual attitude to the phenomena of the world, a type of practical behaviour, or even a philosophy of life. These, however, are only impenetrable and aimless generalizations which lose all power of definition when it comes to identifying the shades of opportunistic arse-licking with which we are concerned. The concept of opportunism falls prey to oversimplification if the sights are set on the opportunistic arse-licker, whether he is considered as careless, stupid, eccentric or, purely and simply, a scoundrel or thoroughly bad person.

Little is gained by this approach because it does not take us behind the scenes of opportunistic arse-licking, that is, to the forces which impel the arse-licker towards his goal and which ultimately determine whether his conduct deserves approval or disapproval. Let us therefore change tack and search for these goal-directed forces without subjecting them to an examination as to the motives.

The most important thing, in my view, is not the indefinable search for happiness but man's insatiable and hence so seductive hunger for power, be it on a small or large scale. People have always tried to achieve power by any means, fair or foul, including opportunistic arse-licking – which, if successful, they use again in order to achieve more power. Competition and ambition are closely connected with this. The purpose of competition is gain, and in this context opportunistic arse-licking can go as far as covert violence. Ambition as a driving force aims at prestige, in which case arse-licking takes the form of actions designed to give pleasure to, and elicit praise from, those whose judgement one appreciates. We must also list the striving for leisure and for the enjoyments of the senses as causes of arse-licking, particularly where people are not in a position to achieve these through their own efforts and exertions. I could continue in this vein, referring to such diverse concepts as wealth and honour, high-handedness and arrogance, thrift, belief, heresy and suspicion, but by going on in this pompous manner I would risk ignoring the discretion inherent in opportunistic arse-licking.

Those who desire advantages, support or benefits cannot avoid having to ask for them, however loudly their deeds may speak for themselves. They must take opportune actions, even if this offends their self-love, self-conceit, sense of rank or vanity. These qualities must be overcome and replaced with ambition as a driving force of opportunistic arse-licking. But cowardice also plays its part, because with ambition as with cowardice discretion is the be-all and end-all. Without going at great length into whether cowardice is the mother of cruelty, as Michel de Montaigne thought, or whether ambition is rooted in men's hearts, as Blaise Pascal believed, I will move into the world of music, which is close to me, in order to demonstrate the linkage between ambition and cowardice in opportunistic arse-licking, by means of an example.

I see before me the unique figure of Richard Wagner. Being a brilliant composer, Wagner revolutionized music. As dozens of academic or popularizing biographies show, he found himself in some extremely difficult situations in his time. Not only did he have many enemies but in other respects too his life was not, to put it mildly, a bed of roses. As the man of action that he was, he used every opportunity that arose to gain recognition for his work, and also to improve his often precarious personal circumstances, for which he certainly cannot be blamed. The only question is: how?

Wagner's relationship with the highly sensitive King Ludwig of Bavaria, who was infinitely enthusiastic about his work, is well known. Everything that has been written about this, whether or not correct in detail, suggests that Wagner resorted to opportunistic arse-licking to secure the help of his royal patron – about whom personally he did not care a hoot – in order to realize his ambitious projects, for example the establishment of the festival theatre in Bayreuth.

This example from Wagner's eventful and difficult life, which should on no account be interpreted as blame, may be complemented by another. In every biography of the great composer a more or less lengthy chapter is devoted to the 'Mathilde Wesendonk affair'. Some biographers emphasise that this was a pure friendship between the married

Wagner and the married Mathilde Wesendonk. Others argue that it was a love affair between two kindred souls, while others again speak of a liaison laden with romanticism and devotion which inspired Wagner in his work on *Tristan and Isolde*. Nobody knows what really went on, but such are the accounts based on existing letters and Wagner's not always truthful autobiography. For whatever reason, Mathilde's husband, the wealthy Otto Wesendonk, had to watch all the joys and sorrows of the two transfigured creatures and was, moreover, allowed to finance what Wagner called his temporary 'asylum' in Zurich. Clearly, Wagner's selfishness, attested in all situations of his life, was not only so enormous that he refused to show his patron the smallest sign of gratitude, but it was also shored up, as in the case of Ludwig, the fairy-tale king, by opportunistic arse-licking.

I will sumbit only one piece of evidence for my view: a letter from Wagner to Otto Wesendonk, in which the attentive reader can hear the language of the self-centred opportunist. Dated 24 August 1859, the letter runs as follows:

> For God's sake, dearest friend, do not consider it an insult if I implore you to take back the money you have offered me. – I cannot in all honesty accept a loan, for I know my situation – which will probably never change. Even less must I accept a gift from you, to whom I already owe

such considerable sacrifices, or – let me assure you – from anyone else. Please accept my thanks for your kind disposition and my warmest good wishes.

Most sincerely yours,
Richard Wagner

I do not wish to belittle the greatness of Wagner's work as a musician by this compressed report of an episode from his life. Far from it. I shall not be prevented from loving and admiring his music even by his undiluted opportunism in using the Jewish conductor Hermann Levi for the first performance of *Parsifal* in spite of his own rabid anti-Semitism. We must draw a line between the baseness of the man and our respect for the artistic genius. For it is in the nature of opportunistic arse-licking, whether overt or stealthy, on the one hand to demand and accept favours and on the other hand to drag up unpleasant facts.

I have no intention of playing the part of prosecutor in relation to this, surely congenital, human proclivity called opportunism – no, I am talking specifically about opportunism as allied with arse-licking. In the world of music we find many other composers revered by posterity, who made use of opportunism in the course of their lives, either according to their nature or out of necessity, stooping as low as arse-licking in some cases.

Let us only recall the incomparable Jacques

Offenbach, the Jewish cantor's son, who furthered his career by sucking up either to the financial sponsors of his theatre or to his librettists, until his music became world-famous. He did not even hesitate to become a Catholic in order to marry a strictly Catholic lady called Herminie, so that her uncle, an impresario, might take him under his wing. Or let us remember the ever unfortunate Gustav Mahler – a formidable conductor drifting from one opera house to the next, and an awesome composer misunderstood and attacked by his contemporaries – who also converted to Catholicism in order to be appointed director of music at the Vienna Court Opera.

It is not for us to indict the opportunism of people who show off what they have and what they are able to do, particularly if they have given the world some unique and lasting values. It is only when they go too far, lowering themselves to the ignominy of arse-licking, that the wise Pascal's maxim becomes applicable: 'One must know when to doubt, when to be certain, and when to submit.'

We would be doing an injustice to those who continually or occasionally behave in an opportunistic manner if we were to overlook the fact that opportunism speaks many languages and plays many parts. Astonishingly, it is indeed overlooked in most cases despite the obviousness of this type of human behaviour, because in most judgements the only factors weighed up and contrasted are self-interest and unselfishness.

Opportunism

Even opportunism of the arse-licking kind should not be seen as an unmitigated defect. We must grant that at one level this pattern of behaviour serves to satisfy a reciprocal *need for recognition* in the arse-licker and in others. On the one hand, the recognition achieved through opportunism allows the arse-licker to admire himself for having aroused, as he assumes, the admiration of the others. On the other hand, his opportunism pleasantly gratifies the need for recognition of the other person or persons. The result is a tacit understanding, without which social existence would not be possible.

Enough of interpretation. Let us consider another example from the world of music which reveals the mutual need for recognition as the incentive of opportunism in its many facets. At the onset of winter, allegedly for the benefit of the art, we are informed that in the coming spring, summer and autumn seasons festivals of music – old, new, resurrected or future – will be held here, there and everywhere. Preparatory meetings of cultural panels, artistic directors, impresarios, financial advisers, and experts in tourism and public relations take place in order to enable music to be played somewhere or other for seven days. While in one place tarted-up festival committees put their money on great crowd-pulling works played by great crowd-pulling artists, in another place unknown pieces unearthed by competent excavators are banked on. Leaving all idealistic eyewash on one side, the emphasis is on the promotion of tourism and the opportunistic need for recognition.

The latter even affects the appointment of the conductor. Although it is common knowledge that Herr Schmitz is able to conduct Brahms's 'Second' perfectly well, we must have M. Dupont. After all, M. Dupont has not only conducted most successfully in Lucerne, Florence and Kassel but, what is more, he also thrills the audiences with his elegant interpretation, his gestures and his blue tails – so: M. Dupont, please! But M. Dupont already has nineteen other engagements for the season, and he is not prepared to conduct Haydn's *Creation*, which is on the programme. All right, then: we shall take the opportunity of M. Dupont being free on the days on which we would like to have him, and we shall grovel and allow him, in God's name, to conduct Beethoven's 'Ninth'.

Thus, in sociological terms, the need for recognition reveals itself as a pattern of behaviour consisting of opportunism, complacency, vanity and idle triviality. Placed in the middle of social – or, in our example, socio-musical – life, the behavioural pattern of opportunism is despised where it outstrips and/or obscures the substantive issue through the manifestation of arse-licking. However, where opportunism keeps within the limits of the purely human and personal it always remains the norm.

VI

Interlude

Not a question of character

🐘

Before continuing to explore the ins and outs of arse-licking and its further ramifications, I must explain why I am not discussing this human phenomenon simply under the heading of 'character' or 'characteristic', and why I do not simply say that this or that person engaged in grovelling has a weak, difficult, malignant, noble, good or bad character. After all, the easiest way of characterizing people is to list their positive qualities and their faults.

But how can one classify arse-licking, particularly if one does not want to go in for the facile apriorism of regarding it from the outset as bad, reprehensible or selfish?

Characterology, the scientific study of character, is not short of classifications: Voltaire and Lessing are characterized as 'sanguine'; Kant, Hume and Darwin as 'phlegmatic'; Dostoyevsky, Lenau and Grillparzer as 'nervous'; Rousseau and Kierkegaard as 'sentimental'; Danton, Proudhon and Gambetta as 'choleric'; Michelangelo, Napoleon and Nietzsche as 'passionate'; and so on. As a sociologist I can only regard such typifications as expressions of moods, or emanations of the inner and outer life. If I wanted to establish arse-licking as a characteristic I would therefore have to apply the criteria provided by the various branches of psychology.

That, however, seems inappropriate to me. For psychology, in dealing with human character, takes as its starting point constant attitudes, perspectives and modes of behaviour, either innate or acquired, which essentially and fundamentally determine the specificity of an individual. But I cannot accept this as far as arse-licking is concerned, which, as I have already explained, I consider above all as a purposive ideology. On the one hand, arse-licking is not a 'constant' trait but one that changes according to circumstances; and on the other hand, it is not something that 'fundamentally' determines the specificity of an individual. Arse-licking depends on circumstances and occurs sporadically in the life of a person, whether choleric, sanguine or of any other type. From a sociological point of view it is unintegrated, incoherent and inconsistent, whether in its rudimentary form, its moderate form, or its highly developed intellectual form. Unlike a personal characteristic, arse-licking – seen as an interpersonal relationship based on actions, or as a *pattern of behaviour* – cannot be grasped in terms of its properties. Arse-licking occurs in many different variations, which we shall explore in the following chapters.

VII

Lies, Hypocrisy, Flattery
The basics of deception

Olaf Gulbransson: In front of the scenes

Like all of us, I have told more than one lie in my life, at least of the kind commonly dismissed as a 'white lie'. Many of my less whopping lies occurred in my youth. To avoid having to go to school I would pretend to have a cough; to replace my swimmming lesson with a visit to the cinema I would show my mother a swimsuit soaked under the water tap; to be able to hang out in the streets instead of going to my piano lesson I would tell my parents that my piano teacher was ill; and many more such trifles. Naturally I was always caught lying and properly punished. My mother would accompany my misconduct with the exclamation: 'The boy is lying again'. My father, spanking my backside, would cite an ominous proverb to the effect that nothing under the sun could remain hidden for ever, which did not impress me very much.

In my student years I also told my parents many a lie. While I was studying at Cologne University I led them to believe that I also had to attend lectures at the University of Bonn and needed a motor cycle – which I was given and promptly drove into a tree rather than to the University in Bonn. To escape the dull city of

Cologne and parental supervision, I lied to them that first-class law could be studied only at the University of Freiburg. Once there, in order to supplement my always inadequate monthly allowance, I lied to my parents that I had to buy whole rows of textbooks. Thanks to many tricks like these I was able to lead the kind of merry student life that was still possible in those days when one was not under pressure to do well.

There was no absolute necessity for these and similar juvenile follies supported by lies. But things changed when the Nazi hordes drove me out of Germany and I had to seek refuge as an emigrant in distant Australia. In order to get there one needed an entry permit. This was not easy to obtain because Australia did not want to admit academics, scholars and professional people, but only skilled workers and craftsmen. At that time I was scraping along as a waiter in Paris, and so I conceived the idea of passing myself off to the Australian authorities as a trained chef. For that purpose, however, various certificates were needed, of which the history graduate Silbermann naturally had none. With deportation from France imminent, I roamed the writing rooms of reputable hotels, pinching their notepaper and fabricating first-class references, in a disguised handwriting and with forged signatures, recommending me as an expert chef. It was as such that I received the Australian entry permit, and I should add that this lie also proved useful for my first job as a kitchen manager in Sydney.

Lies, Hypocrisy and Flattery

The purpose of this report is to clarify from the outset the difference between lying and cheating, and to illuminate the problem under discussion in terms of the statement by Pierre Corneille, the French classicist: 'How useful is the art of lying at the right time'.

The problem facing us consists in connecting the behavioural pattern called 'lying' with that called 'arse-licking'. Whatever little homilies on the topic of 'lying' we hear or read – along the lines of 'lies have short wings', 'a liar will not be believed even if he tells the truth', or 'the truth will out' – nowhere do we find even the slightest hint in the direction of arse-licking. The proverbial phrases I have just cited are always based on the moral principle of 'thou shalt not lie', which, incidentally, does not occur among the Ten Commandments. Sociological thinking here comes up against a wall which we cannot hope to penetrate unless we first consider the general concept of 'lying' with its variable qualities.

To make matters deliberately simple, I assume that 'lying' is a social action with the purpose of consciously concealing, distorting and falsifying the truth. On this assumption we first encounter that almost unselfish kind which can be called a happy lie or a joke. This involves an element of surprise, for instance if I invite guests and tell them that nobody else is coming, knowing that I have also invited other guests to surprise them. Such a happy lie, unconnected to any kind of arse-licking, provides the foundation for many a play, from Johann Strauss's *Fledermaus* to Georges Feydeau's sparkling comedies of manners.

The semi-official lie, which often contains a grain of truth, however small, or at least a plausible supposition, is used either to please and benefit, or to criticize, reprimand and condemn, a person or a group. This mild form of lying is often encountered in both written and spoken form. It operates through public announcement, rumour and *on dit*. The semi-official lie is particularly popular with the tabloid press, whispering about marital conflicts, addictions, financial troubles or illnesses of people in the limelight. Here one would like either to sympathize with the people concerned or to join public opinion in order to discredit, disempower or dispossess them. In this area it is hardly necessary for me to cite examples and names. We only need to observe the untruthful 'statements' and corresponding corrections or retractions from the world of politics, economics, the arts or sport that appear at least once a week.

Finally we have to mention the harmful and malicious lie, which is generally despised. This lie does its dirty work by damaging and hurting people. Although it is used in many different ways, the intention is mostly vindictive. 'I'll have revenge, no longer can I bear it', the Queen of Night sings in Mozart's *Magic Flute*, entreating her daughter with a lie to murder Sarastro, the High Priest of light. This kind of lie is truly terrible, cruel, durable and beyond reconciliation.

No arse-licking is needed to bring into circulation the mendacious patterns of behaviour that I have briefly outlined. One can deploy them with one's 'head held high', even if they only serve one's own advantage. This observation is an eye-opener. For although it is universally acknowledged that lying and arse-licking are negative attitudes and should therefore go well together, that is evidently not the case. The answer that lying is a natural phenomenon, while arse-licking is not, is too easy to be taken seriously. To resolve the discrepancy which arises from the fact that lying does not necessarily have to be guided by arse-licking, we have to examine the *nature* of lies.

None of us who has ever told a lie – and who has not – has done so in a vacuum. Behind every lie a small fragment of the truth is hidden. It is part and parcel of the lie that the liar is aware of the truth he is distorting: one always lies in relation to something that one knows. That is why insidious phrases such as 'I don't want to deceive you, I can swear that what I am saying is true' are commonly prefixed to a lie – phrases that one would beware of uttering before a tricky act of arse-licking. If, then, the liar who knows or believes that he knows the truth, deliberately says something different from what he knows or believes, is he not, strictly speaking, lying 'in good faith'? But 'good faith' is a figure of speech which implies reliability, plausibility and sincerity, together with the notion that one's words or deeds obey the truth of what what one is or thinks. This is never the case with lies, and lying therefore always remains within the bounds of 'bad faith', unreliability and dishonesty – which makes it as iniquitous as arse-licking.

But does that mean that every lie is iniquitous and culpable, so that one should never tell a lie? Let us take an example from Germany's not so glorious past. During the murderous era of the Nazis, compassionate people hid persecuted Jews or resistance fighters in their houses. Unexpectedly the bloodthirsty Gestapo arrive, looking for them. What is to be done? Tell the truth or lie? Faced with these brutal henchmen it is actually one's duty to lie – on the one hand for one's own sake, and on the other hand in order to protect the persecuted. Mind you, I do say 'lie', and the lie still remains what it is, namely a deliberately false statement not corresponding to the truth. However, the lie in our present example is honourable, indeed heroic. This demonstrates that truthfulness need not be an absolute duty, as many of our philosophers, led by Kant, maintain. If one lies out of compassion or in order to survive, to oppose barbarism or to comfort the dying, then one lies in good faith in relation to what one believes to be true. But this still does not make lying a virtue, as might be thought. Lying is and remains an offence, a transgression, a disgrace – the only thing lying has in common with arse-licking, while arse-licking itself is not a necessary ingredient of lying.

Very often lying and hypocrisy are mentioned in the same breath. 'He is a liar and a hypocrite' is a well-known exclamation of protest and humiliation uttered by the injured party. Nor do public voices flinch from pillorying those representatives of the people involved in scandals, calling them liars and hypocrites in response to their depositions before committees of enquiry. Are we faced with two different concepts placed side by side, or are the two terms being treated as synonyms? The latter seems to be the case if we consider that there are few true synonyms but plenty of converging ideas, mainly because our ideas are much more imperfect than our language. Obviously hypocrisy is at least close to lying, which may be why the various dictionaries of synonyms, irreplaceable tomes though they are, do not mention it at all. But surprisingly enough, even in the common encyclopedias the head words 'hypocrisy' and 'hypocrite' are either simply missing or followed by brief definitions like: 'hypocrisy' = vice, consisting in pretending to possess feelings or virtues which one does not possess, and 'hypocrite' = a person who pretends to be honest, virtuous, meek, kind, devout, generous, etc. Sometimes there are also references to sanctimoniousness, two-facedness and affectation of sincerity and friendliness.

I confess that these laconic reflections on virtues that people have or pretend to have will not get me very much further in my observation of arse-licking – above all if I think of all the social manifestations to which hypocrisy can be attached: from a hypocritical countenance, a hypocritical tone or manner of speaking, hypocritical deference and hypocritical zeal, to the hypocritical demeanour used in an attempt to hide intrigues. Would it not be better, therefore, to connect hypocrisy with pretence or concealment, particularly as there are enough people around who find it impossible to be straightforward in any situation? But by doing so we would fall victim to a common mistake and be sidetracked from the topic of arse-licking. A person who simply pretends – that is, a person who lacks openness – conceals his opinions and keeps his secrets, whether obeying caution or necessity. The hypocrite, by contrast, surrounds his views with falsehoods, practising deception by words and deeds – until success enables him to drop his mask.

Hypocrisy has always been a means of obtaining wealth, position, attention, importance or favour of the mighty and, furthermore, a means of hurting others and elevating oneself. How far hypocrisy has to resort to arse-licking is clearly seen when it presents itself in the cloak of cheerfulness, affability or good nature. Such operations or customs are used to hide the dangerous qualities of hypocrisy. In fact hypocrisy related to customs and morals is one of the most vicious types of arse-licking. It produces in our society an almost addictive indignation aroused by anything that could impair traditional or self-invented customs.

Wherever there is power, influence and wealth we also see masses of hypocritical arse-lickers seeking out the idols representing these benefits. Science and learning, philosophy, economics and finance, democracy, dictatorship, and not least religion – each of these domains has its Tartuffe, as Molière demonstrated on stage centuries ago. It is not for nothing that 'tartufferie' has come to mean hypocrisy in French. Molière presents the type of sanctimonious hypocrite who believes in nothing and who, armed with crawling submissiveness, stoops to all kinds of baseness. It has been elegantly said that hypocrisy is the homage paid by vice to virtue, but in reality the mere fact that hypocrisy serves the interests and at the same time violates the self-respect of the hypocrite is sufficient reason to call hypocrisy a form of arse-licking.

When, in preparation of this chapter on lying and hypocrisy, I was looking for everyday forms of arse-licking in order to appraise them from a sociological point of view, I chanced, among others, upon the association with *flattery*. This embarrassed me, because I know well enough how susceptible I myself am to flattery – particularly if it relates to my work as a scholar and writer. But what is applause or indeed fulsome praise? Nothing other than cleverly hidden, subtle flattery which, in different ways, satisfies both the person who gives and the person who receives the praise: I receive it as a reward for my merits, while the other person gives it in order to prove his honesty and discrimination. Should I therefore delete it from my inventory of arse-licking?

It would be rash to deny that we have ever been taken in by people who we had been warned were not just flatterers but, in the vernacular, lickspittles and creeps. Although flattery is generally regarded as a false currency, it rides high, above all as a method of satisfying people's vanity. Seen in this light, flattery involves little or indeed no arse-licking, but belongs more or less among the everyday courtesies and is largely free from utilitarian elements. Flattery in general is neither despised nor hated, chiefly because it is rather pathetic and requires no special shrewdness. What is despised and hated, however, is flattery combined with arse-licking. This means that there must be different kinds of flattery. Let us conduct a brief survey.

Flattery as such is commonly understood to mean praise born out of the desire to attract sympathy by being pleasant, obliging and appealing. However, when praise is used for profit it is generally regarded as a base, shameful and odious kind of flattery. There are therefore differences – not only as to whether flattery takes a spoken, written, printed, painted or sculpted form, but also as to whether or not flattering remarks carry the hallmark of arse-licking. One example: a portrait painter who endows his model with a beauty not present in reality is engaged in flattering without deceitful arse-licking. However, it only takes one glance at the statues of emperors, kings and generals who adorn our squares and bridges in heroic postures to realize that their flattering portrayal by the artist as arse-licker does not correspond to their real appearance. A further example: I often used to be invited by a significant scholar known for his meanness, who always offered his guests the cheapest

Algerian red wine in bottles bearing Bordeaux labels. People would politely raise their glasses, smell the red liquid, take a sip, smack their lips appreciatively, and lick the influential host's arse by praising his excellent taste and first-rate knowledge of wine.

We must also mention 'negative' flattery, or the so-called gesture of friendship. Here the intention of arse-licking can be recognized when criticism is invariably introduced by a phrase like 'I'm no flatterer, and I tell you frankly what I think'. How often have I experienced this seemingly adroit flattery when the flattering friend criticized some mistakes in my writings which seemed completely insignificant to me, before citing passages of which, as he well knew, I was particularly proud. Behind this mask of a brave and loyal lover of the truth we find a great many arse-lickers. They are those who allegedly 'mean well' for us, but who in reality are out to 'do well' for themselves.

As a final example of elementary arse-licking by flattery, let us remember those disastrous regimes in which subjects have tried to curry favour with the rulers either by giving them false praise or by calling everything they did something else. If the ruler committed acts of cruelty, he was said to be setting an example; for occasions and activities that deserved censure and blame, he received thanks; if he paid tributes to his enemies, he was said to do so for a quiet life, turning his servility into a sign of superiority; when he gave the impression that he was signing a peace treaty against his will, he was praised for his courage. Flattery lends the unworthy ruler sublime greatness; it gives the unjustified exercise of power its blessing and it wishes villains and wrongdoers happiness and prosperity. If I say that flattery is usually an act of hypocrisy, and hence arse-licking used to subjugate others, then I see the flatterer – regardless of what kind – as a person who misuses his talents and never seeks the truth for its own sake.

Admittedly, just as stimuli and reactions turn into habits, we all love adulation. Nevertheless, we must protect ourselves from those who try to pull the wool over our eyes by crude arse-licking.

VIII

Intrigue and Perfidy
Secret machinations

Pieter Brueghel the Elder: The man with the money bag and his flatterers (1568/69)

Die ghelt te gheuen heeft onder hooghe en slechte En dat hij waer met laet doen syren schat druijpen, Hij cruijct Officien en toint zijnen rechte, Want dick en dunt niet hoe hem sal in gaet cruijpen. ✠

On ne sait comme entrer en vain,
Au trou de il qui damer peut.

6-4

In the process of defining the relationship between lies, hypocrisy and arse-licking I came across suggestions that lies were used by intriguers. This made me prick up my ears because in listing the different manifestations of arse-licking I had not thought of intrigue. Had I overlooked something, or am I on the wrong track? For the sake of sociological circumspection, if nothing else, I must therefore find out whether, and how far, the pattern of behaviour described as intrigue is or is not connected with the pattern of behaviour described as arse-licking.

The word 'intrigue' is never uttered in a vacuum. In everyday usage it always occurs in directive contexts. One speaks of 'conducting or seeing through an intrigue', a 'base, vile, personal or political intrigue', an 'intriguer', exploration of the 'background of an intrigue', etc. But, although in all these cases there is a strong suggestion of villainy, there is no common denominator, no collective meaning, shared by the various forms of intrigue. Special caution is in order, because intrigue can also refer to those elements which propel the plot of a work of literature. In many dramas, comedies and operas (for instance in Rossini's *The Barber of Seville*) a conspiracy of some of the characters against another is an essential part of the story. In other words, seen in a literary or dramaturgical light, the intrigue consists of a sequence of facts and events which create suspense in the audience as to the outcome planned by the author.

The meaning of intrigue as an activity, which is our concern, is a very different matter. Briefly, this type of intrigue is a secret machination designed to secure some advantage or to harm somebody. It is an underhand method, directed like arse-licking towards a certain goal, and therefore a purposive ideology. However, this does not mean that intrigue, necessary or useful as it may be in everyday life, can be included without further ado among the variants of arse-licking. In order to solve the problem we must examine the conditions and social contexts in which intrigue – with or without arse-licking – becomes evident.

Our lives are often invaded by stealthy advisers, whom we may or may not have invited. They have a habit of appearing when they have heard that we are planning to do or not to do something, and they volunteer, under the guise of sincerity, opinions on the matter. When these opinions are charged with criticism, reprimand or praise ('you did the right thing') they reveal the intention of starting an informal intrigue, which is inevitably connected with the kind of arse-licking which we have identified as flattery –

particularly as human beings do not give anything as generously as advice.

Another incentive of intrigue is the human attribute we call envy or, somewhat less harshly, resentment. To avoid premature or far-fetched conclusions it is necessary to define the semantic field of 'envy'. Envy is a form of annoyance, aversion or even hatred. It encompasses feelings opposed to the well-being, happiness and success of other people. It compels the emotions and the intellect to view the physical, social and mental advantages of others with bitterness, and with melancholy. Generally such acute bouts of covetousness reveal a mean and repulsive nature, which is regarded as more or less reprehensible. Envy, not to be confused with competitiveness, is always annoyed by the well-being, success or merits of others, which it tries to belittle.

It is not for nothing that Adolph von Knigge, my companion in these reflections, exclaims: 'Do not praise your good luck too loudly. Do not display your greatness, riches and talents too brightly. For people can rarely bear such superiority without protest and envy.' We must note that envy as a mental faculty has the power to misdirect human behaviour. Depending on the circumstances, such behaviour may include the combination of intrigue and arse-licking, which causes not only happiness but also sorrow, misfortune and suffering and, generally speaking, exploits the weaknesses of others. Merely to say 'I know this man: he is my friend and he is worth more than all of you put together' sets in motion an intrigue, the envious panacca beloved by braggarts, grudgers and schemers. The saying that it is better to provoke envy than pity is thus stood on its head.

If we speak of envy we must not forget *jealousy*, the envious annoyance generated by the advantages or profits of others. Jealousy is usually mentioned in connection with affairs of love and affection, signifying the fear that the loved one does not reciprocate one's love and prefers somebody else. Jealousy is said to be the 'sister of love', but it can also target the honour, dignity, talents or wealth of another person. Whenever it arises its bitter rancour ruins the enjoyment of life.

However, although jealousy is usually accompanied by envy, engaging in intrigue does not do it much good. For intrigue, highlighting as it does the intriguer's own fantasies and suppositions, has no power to convince. However tragic the effects of jealousy may be, its violent outbreak can at most entice the jealous person into intriguing, but can never be the primary incentive of the evil deed.

Everybody knows how horrifyingly cruel and implacable *revenge* is. In essence it is impelled by the fear of disaster to try to suppress, combat and punish an act of defamation, insult, disrespect, or, in short, humiliation. To achieve this, any method will do – slander, rumour, tale-telling, accusations and also intrigue. But we must ask whether arse-licking is needed for all this. I do not think so, particulary if the revenge is not public but *private*. The nature of private revenge is such that the avenger is always the weaker person. And since his sense of weakness gives him strength, as it were in compensation, the instrument of revenge, which in this context is the intrigue, requires no arse-licking.

Things are different with revenge perpetrated in *public*. In this context any intrigue guided by vindictiveness – whether in politics, economics, the judiciary or the civil service – always carries at least a whiff of what I have shown to be the purposive ideology of arse-licking. Let us illustrate this by a well-known affair of the old days. In May 1895 the English writer Oscar Wilde was sentenced to two years' imprisonment with hard labour for 'acts of indecency with male persons'. It all began with a provocative intrigue on the part of the Marquess of Queensberry, father of the young Lord Alfred Douglas who was a close friend of the homosexual writer. Badly advised and wilfully goaded by Alfred Douglas to sue his father for defamation, Wilde became involved in scandalous court cases which came to exercise the public far beyond the borders of England. Over the whole disastrous affair – from the vindictive intrigue of the Marquess through the court hearings to the conviction of Wilde – hung the thick cloud of the prudish and hypocritical Victorian morality and ideology. And, as the records show, this 'public' was treated to all available tricks to lubricate, as it were, the outbreak of its hypocrisy.

I could list other more or less well-known examples of the coincidence of intrigue, arse-licking and public revenge, including the 'Dreyfus affair', a scandal in French politics between 1894 and 1914. In this case of espionage, involving all sorts of intrigues, a public was created and exploited for the purpose of taking revenge on the militarist faction on the one hand and on the anti-militarists on the other. A further intention, given the fact that Dreyfus was a Jew, was to stir up anti-Semitism.

But enough of evil and its history. As we have seen, intrigue does not necessarily occur in conjunction with arse-licking. Basically, it is a pathetic kind of cleverness which resorts to arse-licking when it sees a prospect of profit. There can be no doubt that some people simply find it impossible to go about anything in a straightforward manner. All their enterprises, even the most innocent, are tainted by intrigue. Even if we regard this bad habit – to put it mildly – as mere ruse, trickery, *schadenfreude* or duplicity, its aim is always to get more than one already has – with or without the humiliation of arse-licking.

In my scholarly forays into literature on the subject of 'intrigue' I have sometimes come across 'perfidy', a sonorous term only rarely used in colloquial language today. I asked myself whether perfidy is the same as, or a variety of, intrigue. I soon discovered that it is neither the one nor the other, when one speaks of a perfidious woman, a perfidious lover, a perfidious friend or perfidious Albion. If, in a dictionary, we find

the equivalents 'malice,' 'deceitfulness', 'faithlessness'
and 'baseness', the idea of meanness and wickedness
may provide a bridge to intrigue.

However, when we speak of a perfidious smile or
silence, a perfidious oath or trick, is there not more at
stake than merely gaining an advantage by playing the
game of intrigue? Indeed there is because, as the interpretation of each of these concepts – whether desig-
nated as malice, deceitfulness, faithlessness or baseness
– shows, behind each of them there is an intention,
namely the intention to harm or hurt. This in turn
means that perfidy itself consists of the intention to do
evil and the abuse of any kind of trust. As a deception
involving the entire person, perfidy always hides
behind an attractive and charming appearance – that
is, behind arse-licking, which is the only thing it has in
common with intrigue.

IX

Love

Mightier than man

Franz Kafka: Supplicant and high patron

Love

I hesitated for a long time before discussing love, this eternal truth, in the gloomy and uncomfortable context of arse-licking. By doing so, am I not violating the feeling that guides the soul to what it perceives as good, beautiful or true, and am I not trampling underfoot the impulse of the heart that attracts us to another person, our profound affection for people and things? I fear I am. But if I consider everything that people do to this all-embracing essence of humanity, my fear departs and, adopting Goethe's maxim, I examine that which is and not that which pleases. Besides, is it not a marvellous thing to advance into the realm of love, and was it for nothing that the greatest thinkers of all times contemplated love because they were hit by Cupid's arrow, as we all are once in a while?

In antiquity many philosophers originally regarded love only as a physical desire of the senses. They placed this precious good on a pedestal which is to this day surrounded by a thicket of love stories in words, pictures or music that are served up to us as if they were love itself. But already Socrates, Plato, Aristotle and Plutarch saw in love far more sensitive and sub-lime emotions. Plato's *Symposium* reads like a standard work on idealized emotional love transcending the senses, which on earth appears only as an imperfect attempt or pale reflection.

Sketchy as my remarks must remain, let us now move on to the end of the Middle Ages, where we find the philosophers Descartes and Spinoza, who regard love as a violent passion which can be controlled only by reason, whereby it is transformed into a lucid and happy consciousness. We must not pass over mystics such as St Augustine or Pascal, for whom all love derives from the love of God, since there is only one love, which is the ultimate explanation of everything. We must also mention Schopenhauer and Nietzsche, who saw love as a trap set by the genius of the species to ensure that life continues. And finally let us hear Herbert Spencer, the English social philosopher, who examined the components of love. These, in his opinion, are: affection, admiration, desire for recognition, self-respect, pleasure of possession, enjoyment of a wide-ranging freedom of action, and effusive sympathy.

What fine words. But is this not a rather poor and hackneyed vocabulary? Even poets often despair of being able to find the right expressions for the gestures and symptoms of love, instead of constantly repeating themselves and becoming monotonous. Let alone philosophers, who do not favour dramatic representations. I for my part – at the risk of being considered old-fashioned, and without going into psychological or psychoanalytical motives – regard love as an immeasurably noble inspiration for the lovers. Thus I differ from those naturalists who, in their pursuit of reality, see love as a thin disguise of, and a prelude to, the self-assertion of desire.

We must break off these incomplete speculations by admitting, however hard we may find it, that love on the one hand arises from instinctual sources and on the other hand pursues an ideal aim. Since these points of view are generally considered as opposites, the interpreters or narrators of love only rarely dare to present more than half the truth, and at the same time they ignore its real social implications.

I am concerned that my comments could take us on a tightrope walk between love and desire, of which arse-licking can only be an alien and therefore irrelevant or even nonsensical by-product. This, for instance, is the case with topics such as 'love and solitude', 'love and the supernatural', 'love and death', 'love of love', 'love and failure' and, not least, 'love as a semblance of morality', which are so popular with the adherents of ethics. We must keep clear of this kind of speculation to avoid being sidetracked from love, as it occurs in everyday life, to those depths of being which are not accessible to empirical knowledge. If I venture to bring the sweet affliction of love within hailing distance of arse-licking I must beware of sentimentality, and I cannot simply describe love as an experience that opens the soul to the most gentle emotions and makes human beings spiritual.

After all, so far we are not even sure whether arse-licking, in whatever form, actually comes into play as a means of either attaining or destroying love. Nor – and most importantly, in my view – are we sure of its object. Is it love itself? That is hardly possible if we recall the introduction to this chapter. Nevertheless, we can recognize in everyday behaviour at least *hints* of arse-licking, be it for the purpose of attaining or of destroying love. Whether this is successful, in a positive or negative sense, need not trouble us any more than the question whether the manipulators are aware of their own arse-licking. Let me briefly list some of these entanglements, useful or detrimental, which we ourselves have probably experienced as lovers.

Let us start with that period of confusion in which letters, promises, longings, entreaties, tears and disappointments are the order of the day. Tender sighs or miserable slanders are used to obtain favours. Rash promises of marriage are lightly given, behind which jealousy and infidelity may already raise their ugly heads. Charm, seduction, flattery and curiosity are tested out to satisfy greed, vanity or sensuality. Other, and more subtle, strategies are: services rendered without major demands in return; displays of openness and gentleness without a sign of weakness; zest without sugariness or recklessness; modesty without timidity; physical agility; vulnerability; and entertaining amorous waffle.

To avoid misunderstanding, this selection can be amplified by some aphorisms to emphasize that I am not trying to expose those acts of arse-licking, whether binding or destructive, small or large, which affect lovers *from outside*, but only those that take place *within* a loving relationship. On this topic we find many pertinent statements, uttered either by ordinary people or by profound intellects, such as:

- There are many remedies against love, but none is infallible.
- There are very few people who are not ashamed of having loved each other once they have stopped doing so.
- There is only one love, but there are a thousand different images of it.
- The less you love the more likely you are to be loved.

The purity of such assertions bars the gate to arse-licking in matters of love as it manifests itself in the relationship between two individuals described as a 'couple'. If this is so – and if it is true, as Voltaire said, that of all the passions love is the strongest since it affects at one and the same time the head, the heart and the body – then we must ask ourselves where love's *power of resistance* comes from. From mythological or religious inspiration or from an enigmatic romantic notion of love, which Shakespeare said was its own interpreter? I consider this an extravagant question leading us away from dreams about love which, although they have no object, consume or weaken the heart.

Discussing the topic of 'love' in relation to the constellation called 'the couple', we step straight into the
centre of those eternal human situations in which fate
and inevitability play a significant part. What we need
to discover is whether this inevitability includes the
purposive ideology of arse-licking in one form and
alignment or another, and whether its intrusion into
the centre of a human condition will be crowned with
success or failure.

Whenever we come close to a human condition
such as love we apprehend a microcosm of human
existence, that is, a microcosm in which human existence crystallizes. On the one hand this apprehension
presupposes a recognition of how love, in the microcosm, becomes *independent*, whereby both its impulses
and its modes of being are spiritualized, with an exalt-
ing or degrading effect. On the other hand it is necessary to realize that in the microcosm love also becomes
socialized, insofar as it is brought into contact with one
of the foundations of human social existence. Love
floating freely in a vacuum is not a subject for representation but, at best, only for contemplation. It is a
misunderstanding of the tension between the two
processes – the drive towards independence and the
drive towards socialization – to insist that the social
aspect of love derives from the sexual, when everyday
reality shows that the sexual aspect of love makes use
of the social. We see this quite clearly when novelists
or dramatists, philosophers, psychologists or sociolo-
gists in their reflections take so-called 'love at first

sight' as their premise – and cannot say anything further. For in this case the couple is just as incapable of
embodying the microcosm of love as it would be if one
took the equation of love and death or, in our context,
of love and arse-licking as the starting point.

Those observing the game of lovers in everyday
reality sidestep this complicated situation by labelling
it with available adjectives: for example, ideal, true,
erotic or emancipated love; or destructive, seductive,
presumptuous and indeed arse-licking love. However,
such indicators appeal to more or less linear emotional
impulses which are only justified when, faced with the
spectacle of the couple, one speaks about love in general terms and simply as an emotion. This approach
based on sensory perception is adopted not only by
poets, or experts in psychology, but also by those who
live in a more or less close relationship to the couple
and who take a larger or smaller degree of interest in
them. In the process, emotional and other elements
are read into, or deduced from, those workings of love
illustrated by the couple which go beyond what can be
grasped and demonstrated in reality – including,
among others, arse-licking. This, however, corresponds no more to the rational events than do the
sexological factors which might be attributed to, or
uncovered in, the love which is active between the
couple.

Couples, like love itself, are not constructs or artificial figures. They are placed within, and exposed to,
situations that endow them with *forces* without which

they would be hollow puppets. As we cannot record all these forces here we must restrict ourselves to briefly listing the most important, noting that they overlap and often even merge with one another.

1 In the first place is the *thematic force*. Every situation contains a dynamic impulse which is embodied in a person or, as in our case, in two persons. This developmental force – as for instance with classical lovers like Romeo and Juliet or Tristan and Isolde – can be seen as an elementary one. It is suited to directing the course of the confusions which arise from the point of departure. In doing so it can be rooted equally well in misjudgement, mistaken identities, fear, ambition, class distinctions, arse-licking or, naturally, love. It can have many different consequences, ranging from cabals to happy endings

2 In order to acquire contours, the thematic force needs an obstacle or resistance: the *opposing force*. This does not involve a third person introducing personal rivalry, but resistance between the lovers themselves. Such is the case when the couple's love is exceeded by differences in birth, class, wealth or education, and also when their personal ability to unfold and develop freely and harmoniously is hampered. In such situations, too, arse-licking can be used.

3 The value of the desired person certainly also plays a part in creating a couple. The idea of this value is

the *evaluative force*. It usually joins the thematic force in adumbrating a craved happiness. This may well go beyond the microcosm of love. Wherever the evaluative force appears symbolized by the same person, happiness is sought and found – depending on the situation – in salvation or death, self-sacrifice, religious illumination, wealth or fulfilment of a longing. It is evident that arse-licking, or even a mere hint of it, has no place here.

4 Like all interpersonal relations, the dynamic of the situation called 'couple' demands a balance, particularly when it is marked by indecision, uncertainty, and disrupting or hopeless circumstances. It befits this *compensating force* to create an equilibrium by assigning good or bad elements to the situation, promoting the object of desire, or preventing misfortune. It is mostly when a couple breaks up that the compensating force gathers all the other forces and leads them towards their goal without a shadow of arse-licking.

My description of the processes at work in love and in the couple is by no means intended to be an abstract analysis of the forces which inflame and encourage the microcosm of lovers, at the same time producing and integrating resistance against arse-licking. What I want to demonstrate here is that in contemplating the couple we must reckon with certain forces operating in conjunction with real human situations. Time and again people within a constellation determined by love are controlled by the forces which determine the situation itself: and the situation becomes more powerful than the people. A mere word or gesture issuing from the compensating force is enough to disturb the equilibrium between the lovers and to lead to a happy or unhappy ending. We can all find ourselves in situations in which one participant or other will mobilize opposing forces which will guide our fate. We either refrain from acting or we try to direct the situation by foiling an action, or, without the slightest ulterior motive of arse-licking, we become aware of the driving forces that I have demonstrated.

It would therefore seem to be the case that, in respect of love as an 'eternal truth' and the couple as an 'eternal type', compelling forces preclude arse-licking, or even a mere hint of it, as I have repeatedly suggested. However, this pleasing result can be countered by saying that in my reflections I have been guided too much by feeling as a starting point and intellectualization as a possible destination: I could be accused of omitting the representation of the love embodied in the couple as an *aesthetic emotion*. We must indeed address this issue, particularly as it could lead us to areas open to arse-licking.

We need to remember that aesthetic emotion is no sentiment *sui generis*: it is neither unique, nor direct, nor constant. Rather, it takes the form of one of many specific sentiments, each of which can become aesthetic in perception – insofar as it is represented under certain conditions. The question is what those 'certain conditions' are under which an emotion – in our present context arse-licking – will become aesthetic and thereby determine the social and cultural identity of the phenomenon. We are thus concerned with *expressions of feelings* taking place between the lovers, who embody love, by way of socially and culturally acquired values and tensions. The 'conditions' in question become 'circumstances' which, owing to the ambiguity of being and seeming, provide at least an opportunity for arse-licking.

Of the ambiguous and antithetical circumstances which can provide scope for arse-licking expressions of feelings the following may be listed:

- *Pleasure* and *displeasure* can produce expressions of feelings in which opposites like well-being and anxiety, joy and horror interact.
- The *real* is opposed to the *unreal*, the unreal being the counterfeit, the insincere, the artificial.
- *Interest* and *disinterestedness* come to the fore depending on whether the loving process reaches the level of passion or is restrained.
- *Truth* and *deception* are in opposition if no absolute significance is attributed to the loving process.
- *Presence* and *absence* are interrelated if the loving process takes things for granted which in reality are no longer present.

The extent to which arse-licking can be introduced into these tensions is difficult to determine, particularly as we are only dealing with possibilities. For the rest, where an unquantifiable amount of love is still present, one or other of the partners will try to overcome the conflict resulting from arse-licking by emotional means which are not understood in the arse-licking process itself.

With reference to the central topic of our reflections we must stress once more that arse-licking as a *purposive ideology*, directed towards positive or negative goals, cannot be linked either with love as an eternal truth or with the couple as an eternal type, neither of which can be made a transitory object of absolute or specific emotions. As Nietzsche said, 'what is done for love is always beyond good and evil.'

X

Family Life
The gateway to happiness

Alfred Kubin: Adoration (*c*. 1900)

After the previous chapter, entitled 'Love', I could imagine myself being accused of deception by straying from the topic of arse-licking. My reply is that I would have been guilty of an unpardonable mistake if I had not also introduced one area of life which – since love is one of the few eternal truths – is more powerful than arse-licking. The tune of arse-licking, which is generally regarded as discordant, had to be provided with a counterpoint, so as to highlight its invariably all-too-human quality. The sociologist in particular, as an observer, analyst and helper in important matters concerning the entire society, must never fall prey to one-sidedness, seeing only the bad, the evil and the damnable in our world. He must also consider the good, the useful, the praiseworthy. And that is how I propose to continue in investigating the suitability or unsuitability of arse-licking for the family. We must be clear that the misuse of arse-licking does not abrogate the permitted use of this art.

The family, a grouping made up of father, mother and children, is the most elementary and most natural of human bonds. In the course of the centuries its structure has been democratized: an absolute monarchy has become a democratic one. The father is still regarded as the head of the family, but he no longer holds such far-reaching powers as he once did. The woman in her turn is no longer the incompetent she used to be taken for; she is no longer obliged to obey her husband, but is expected to carry her share of the burdens in the marriage partnership to the best of her ability. The specific features and consequences of this general rule are governed by the state which has established special family ministries, by the legislature which has enacted specific family laws, by official and semi-official family experts, and by dozens of private agencies for counselling, support and protection. The high value of the family for the welfare and well-being of the population as a whole is undisputed.

It is not surprising that all the different human sciences, including sociology, take an interest in that fundamental institution called 'the family'. Research into the 'sociology of the family' has by now assumed immeasurable proportions. Its topics range from the creation of the family, its functionality and dysfunctionality and its organization and disorganization, through marriage structures, monogamy and the relationship of husband and wife, to the division of labour, extramarital relations and divorce. In my endeavours to provide information on the human fact of arse-licking I am neither able nor willing to address problems of this kind, which are certainly relevant to society, but which do not offer any insight into the

everyday events that take place between men and
women in a family, be it under the shelter of marriage
or of an unmarried partnership. My concern is not to
demonstrate the preservation or destruction of the
institution of the 'family' by arse-licking: I am concerned with *family life*, and with discovering what
motives may be hidden behind arse-licking, in whatever form, were it to raise its head in the context of
family living.

If one speaks of family life in its ideal form, one
expects it to be marked by a harmonious climate.
With the exception of spiteful people, all couples unit-
ing to live as a family share this resolution. In the
bosom of the family, runs the seemly phrase, you will
find homely warmth and security. People may well
wish to maintain this lovey-dovey situation, but a life
without frictions and quarrels, a life without conflicts,
has yet to be found.

Nevertheless, people of good will and family sense
will always seek ways and means to resolve conflicts,
even if these are only emotional. However banal it
may sound, the motto of family life is: 'I want to have
peace and quiet'. To settle unavoidable conflicts which
disrupt the peace of family life, plenty of well-meaning advice is given by counselling services and in particular by popular magazines directed at parents and
families. If one examines their drift one soon realises
that most of their advice goes in the direction of
conciliation by admonitions which honour non-
committalness more than reason. One directive may

follow the maxim 'health is a blessing that money cannot buy', while another may insist on the golden rule that 'charity begins at home', not to mention such vapid commonplaces as 'once bitten, twice shy' or 'more haste, less speed'. It is logical that such general statements leave no room for arse-licking. After all, the objective is to smooth over a possible crisis in family life and not to soil something valuable by a method such as arse-licking which is generally regarded as humiliating.

The success rate of the organizations for assistance and counselling, in which churches and charities, social workers, psychotherapists and self-styled societies for the protection of the family participate, has been, as far as we know, small. Otherwise, why would there have been justified complaints for many years that in Germany every third marriage ends in divorce, that people are getting married less and less and later and later, and if at all, only because of the tax relief? Have things come to such a pass that marriage and family life are regarded, beyond all cold reason, as slavery, which is how August Strindberg presents them in his stage plays? I cannot believe this, even though it is not possible to establish statistically how many 'happy marriages' and 'happy families' there are. Certainly, the recurrent assertion that marriage and the family automatically open the gate to happiness is a myth. What is not a myth, however, is that people at least try to plant and preserve a seed of this mythical longing in everyday reality.

It would be downright naive if not cynical to wallow in idealistic feelings about family life. After all, where do people live together without dissatisfaction and conflict, whether they crave help, advice, attention, entertainment, pleasure, comfort or the fulfilment of any other need? Where do we find a family life which is not impaired by faults and moods that can lead to irritation, coldness, indifference, boredom or even dislike. To avoid such troubles – if one is not to let family life founder on these rocks – arse-licking is entirely appropriate. The question is not whether or not arse-licking is helpful, but how independent it is in relation to the common acknowledgment of an order which does not sanctify it but which endows it with moderation and dignity.

At this point some readers might expect me to describe scenes of crisis or conflict from everyday family life, contrasting them with arse-licking manipulations capable of bringing solutions or peace. I am not going to do that. My inquiry into the sociology of everyday life is neither part of the counselling provided by 'agony aunts' nor a guide to those family soap operas which are meant to make us laugh or cry as they flicker away on television daily. It is simply not possible to tell whether one or other method used to maintain or to ease family life involves any elements of arse-licking, that is, how far overt or hidden arse-licking is employed in the attempt to resolve an oppressive conflict or a simple difference of opinion. Attempts at conciliation, be it the much-praised expedient of talking things over, a friendly discussion, an affectionate embrace, politeness, courteousness, candour or a sense of duty, can but need not be guided by arse-licking.

Things are quite different when family life is subjected to ruling passions, when seduction, dissipation, deception, jealousy, stupidity, lack of attractiveness, extravagance, etc. raise their treacherous heads, in short, when telling the truth and listening to the truth become the prime necessity. Then such praiseworthy qualities as gentleness, kindness or openness are set aside and their place is taken by cleverness, partiality and, above all, pretence. Self-interest, greed, exaggeration and hurt vanity now call the harsh tune and it is inevitable that barefaced lies and feigned emotions should be deployed from the repertory of arse-licking. The question is neither whether the interaction of pretence and arse-licking, applied deliberately or instinctively, leads to success, nor is it the loss of face. What is at issue is the *humiliation* that one side or the other endures owing to the purposeful activity of arse-licking. For this undermines the strength, status and social structure of the at once precious and fragile symbol called 'family life', replacing it with the coercions of a force of nature which often threatens to suffocate people. The art of arse-licking reaches its limits when it tries to produce factors which could destroy human beings.

When the fathers of our Basic Law laid down in paragraph 3.2 that men and women have equal rights, they were very far-sighted. They took the wind out of the sails of feminism's resentful basic principle summed up in the phrase 'agree to disagree', replacing it with the pursuit of harmony, which is necessary for the preservation of the structure and functioning of every society. This provision of the Basic Law was followed by the start of the women's movement, which succeeded more or less in reaching all the pillars of our society, in politics, economics, the judiciary, the administration, the legislature, science, learning and lifestyle. Under the battle cry 'rights for women' an image evolved of men as the enemy, which was designed less to replace patriarchy with matriarchy than to change the attributes of masculinity and femininity, as they also affect family life.

These attributes, in an idealised rather than realistic presentation, lead to stereotypes which make thinking easier. If the stereotypical attributes of femininity are said to be, among others, simplicity, ingenuousness, grace, taste, homeliness and motherliness, then the stereotypes listed for masculinity are, among others, determination, prudence, responsibility, efficiency and authority. When the shift of one or other attribute from the man to the woman and vice versa causes conflicts within the family and a break-up is to be avoided, the use of one of the various forms of arse-licking, particularly *pretence*, seems to me to be justified. What I call pretence has nothing to do, as one might think, with false praise, malicious flattery, feigned stupidity, silence or secrecy, but should be seen as a *demonstration* which can equally well be founded on trust, sincerity, modesty and helpfulness or on compliance, flexibility, caution and distrust.

To be sure, benevolent pretence equipped with decent arse-licking loses its honesty as soon as the embarrassment, degradation or humiliation of a person, or of masculinity or femininity as such, raises its ugly head. For then the upper hand is gained by wishful thinking, impulses and instincts as well as by self-interest and selfishness, with the consequence that either vital or socially binding needs are ignored. However, it is precisely these needs that act as the mainspring of individual behaviour – and it must be emphasized that they always do so in connection with aspirations and desires (a harmonious family life), symbolic notions (masculinity/femininity) and values, including arse-licking, whether one disapproves of it or not.

We will now step out of the close community of family life, in which everyday irritation, misunderstanding, anxiety, opposition, anger, injury or resignation can be alleviated or eliminated without a sign of humiliating arse-licking. For it would be an omission if I looked only at processes *within* one of those groupings which shape our lives. The status, outlook and survival of the nuclear family is also influenced by *external* pressures, such as customs and conventions, styles of life, modes of behaviour or, more broadly, whole social and cultural movements. The equality of man and woman before the law, as laid down by the legislator in this and other countries, is more than just a legal provision: it is a legal principle which once and for all disposed of that outdated plea of sexual difference which served for centuries to support the so-called 'oppression' of women.

I need not explain in detail how hard it was, and still is, to release women from the dead end of the 'three Ks': *Küche, Kinder, Kirche* (kitchen, children, church). Nor do I need to discuss ridiculous secondary phenomena like the crusades of those fellow-travellers and hangers-on of women's liberation who set up courses on 'housework for men', 'ironing for men' or 'spiritual development for women'. There is no doubt that women have found their place in all areas of public life – in politics, economics, the judiciary, culture, sport or science and learning – thanks to laws and regulations from above or to the demonstration of their abilities, with or without the pressure exercised by diverse women's movements, from below. It may sound harsh, and brand me a misogynist, if I say that, as intended, the female sex has derived the greatest profit from the valid principle of equality. The campaigns for equality, public or private, centre on women and not men, or on femininity and not masculinity – which is exploited to best effect in all cases.

This exploitation under the auspices of creating human dignity, whether described as capitalization, utilization or commitment, is not only led by controversial topics such as quotas or adverse career prospects for women. In practice it has also produced

side effects which include a partly overt, partly con-
cealed movement of arse-licking, which affects the
image of woman, or femininity, and thus the family.
My evidence – if it can be called that – is based on
woman as the mover and pivot of a unique technique
called advertising. To avoid vague speculations it is
essential to review briefly how arse-licking in advertising has changed the image of woman.

In the development of commercial advertising we
find, among others, the woman as an object. Originally
her way of presenting herself and competing was
treated sympathetically. At the beginning of our century advertising used the image of the woman to pub-
licize brand names and products, without offering the
woman herself for sale. Slowly the picture changed
and the woman was no longer presented as the ideal of
femininity but was stylized into the ideal woman: she
became an example one followed to improve one's own
image. This was the beginning of advertising by syco-
phantic arse-licking, with sales messages relating above
all to fashionable details and accessories, and creating
the image of the well-groomed woman of good taste,
whose duty and pleasure it seemed to be to enchant.
Arse-licking in and around the image of the woman
now fulfilled two functions: she became the symbol of
a product and an incentive to buy.

After the First World War, the role of the woman
was expanded by social elements, which contributed
noticeably more aggressive elements to her image.
The mythology of the female likeness was resurrected

and with it came tributes which included arse-licking. After the Second World War, efforts to involve the woman in the developing consumer society were intensified by motivational approaches and appeals to the strongest human impulses. Still in brief outline and with the theme of the purposive ideology of arse-licking in mind, we saw instrumentalized eroticism enter the scene as an important method of encouraging buying. The woman now appeared in advertising sparsely clad, but as an impersonal omnipresence composed of scraps of material and female characteristics: she turned into a smile or into pretty hands and legs. At first feminine attractiveness only had to promote an inviting and harmonious image. It was not until the 1960s that the woman actually became a car, a washing machine or a beverage, that is, something that does not draw attention to itself and does not pose the problem of having to make distinctions.

When in the 1960s, connected with pleasant arse-licking, the use and abuse of the woman as an object became too obvious, the successes of advertising visibly declined. In order to survive and to adapt to the extremely rapid social changes, advertising refashioned the woman: the active and busy, free and independent woman became the flavour of the month. The messages and role models which came into being, and penetrated as far as family life, addressed the woman capable of 'managing' herself and others. At the same time, qualifications which existed more or less in reality were praised as an alternative to man.

However, to avoid overdoing things and stirring up conflicts arising from competition, as much homage as ever was paid to feminine beauty. And so we see gorgeous women striving to impersonate the favourites of archetypically handsome and vain men. With subliminal arse-licking swinging from one side to the other, the old dream of the harem is revived, if only by the grotesque repetition of naked or half-naked female beauty.

Since such dazzling beauty, on the one hand, is not a common phenomenon, and since, on the other hand, such a glorification of beauty could all too easily pass over the everyday concerns and traditional values of a conservative public, the 'hidden persuaders' began to coo about the everyday lives of grandmothers and mothers. Like a gang of friends of the family we are led into the kitchen to admire the cooker, the washing machine or the detergents; we watch the neatly dressed mother ironing shirts or feeding her children and cats, or grandmother sipping coffee or conjuring the tastiest instant foods out of paper bags – and all that done cheerfully and with a false smile, the attributes of arse-licking as it is used to compensate for insecurity and untrustworthiness.

The woman created and presented by advertising on billboards, in newspapers, shop windows or television – designed to be a role model and at the same time a turn-on – voices opinions and advice, offers prescriptions for happiness and social standing, lectures, flatters, and exaggerates the actual image of the beautiful woman, the housewife, the mother, the wife or the female companion. Instead of the woman as she really is, we see an image of her which is both close and distant, and which is distorted by arse-licking. Thus the 'eternal feminine' and the many manifestations of its 'mystique' are belittled and reduced to a commercial figure. Where this process penetrates family life it begets the very opposite of true emancipation. The stimulus and employment of arse-licking as a purposive ideology can then become an antidote to unfortunate events rather than their cause.

XI

Education, Louts and the Permissive Society

We only want what is best for you

A. Paul Weber: On the genius's coat-tails (1949)

🐘

So far I have succeeded in deftly restricting my exposition of the art of arse-licking to the world of *adults*. However, I cannot continue to do so without being accused of two wrongs – namely of ignoring, on the one hand, that distinct, much-praised and much-condemned group of young people who embody our hopes for the survival of our society and, on the other hand, those elements of the purposive ideology of arse-licking which arise from the education process and continue into adulthood.

As always, we cannot gain knowledge without a specific object, or fasten on casually dropped phrases like 'that is not done'. Only sensation-seeking advisers proceed in that way, while the sociologist must start from fundamental insights, regardless of what he wants to examine. It is these fundamental insights that I will now briefly outline.

To avoid unnecessarily upsetting my fellow-sociologists, I join them in regarding education as a subsection of socialization, although for those of us concerned with the sociology of everyday life such a distinction amounts to six of one and half a dozen of the other. Basically, the only difference is that in the process of education it is individuals – i.e. parents, relatives or the schools that represent them – who try to impart values, norms and techniques to children and adolescents, while in the process of socialization it is society that transmits and dictates the values, norms and techniques which prevail at a certain time. For our purposes arse-licking can equally well be accommodated in either area as a value, norm or technique.

But things are not so simple if we remember that the process of transmitting the object of our reflections must be based on a relationship, in this particular case the relationship between parents and young people. Let us not fool ourselves: in our youth, when we wanted to evade a prohibition or reservation of our parents, did we not, consciously or instinctively, use the 'technique' of arse-licking, if only by affirming that we 'loved Father best'? And how about our parents with their 'that is good for you' and 'we only want what is best for you' – well-meaning items of arse-licking advanced either reproachfully or benignly?

Nevertheless, there is a difference between the younger and the older generation's way of using the technique: what differs is the *emphasis* behind the expressions. Educators use the technique with a claim to leadership demanding obedience, but this is practically never done by children and adolescents. Furthermore: while the arse-licking behaviour of young people, whether aged five or fifteen, is mostly transparent, the products of socialization (modes of behaviour, performance of practical tasks, ideas, attitudes) which are transmitted by educators, with or without arse-licking, contain vital warnings. Dangers to life are hinted at, underlined or indeed drummed in, together with instructions as to how they can be escaped from, or avoided from the start. In other words, educators try to teach the young to anticipate the consequences of social actions – including arse-licking – or to behave in a moral, logical and rational fashion.

To avoid being distracted by the terrible reports we hear about neglected, homeless and criminal children and adolescents – particularly as they are fortunately not in the majority in the western world – I will assume a relationship between parents and offspring which corresponds to the commonplace image of the 'happy family'. If such happiness is to come to fruition, fondness, affection and concern must be present as a matter of course, and education must be accepted as a duty, which even the legislator has taken in hand in view of its fundamental importance for social life. This duty is marked by rules and expectations which do not simply consist of transmitting and teaching customs, conventions and manners – for example, 'don't speak with your mouth full', 'take your hands out of your pockets', 'brush your teeth' and the like. It is necessary to transmit basic values for human coexistence, such as fidelity, tolerance, pride, forbearance, sincerity, honesty, truthfulness, etc. Both areas of education are governed, on the one hand, by the Biblical commandment 'Thou shalt honour thy father and thy mother' and, on the other hand, by the golden rule that we are all free to decide whether to organize our lives according to the criteria of reason, hope or disappointment.

All this is more easily said than done. For everday life is not characterized by heavenly harmony. Some events, ordinary and extraordinary, stand out from the common flow of life – including education – in terms of both time and content. Whether they are brought to the process of socialization that takes place within the family from outside, or whether they arise from the narrow confines of the family itself, they always create critical situations between the educators and those being educated, which need to be overcome. Despite all the pleasure taken in the comfort of anti-authoritarian education it has remained customary to apply traditional strategies such as reprimands, prohibitions and punishments in many variations and in different degrees of harshness, which more often than not end in a family row, as this agonizing uproar is commonly called.

Now it is very easy to argue about whether rows are an integral part of the family environment, and whether or not human beings actually have a congenital need for rows. Be that as it may, family rows as well as critical situations and the appropriate strategies for overcoming them in the process of education are, to put it mildly, a *strain* on all concerned, parents as well as children. In this context I shall be on my guard against referring to such intangibles as frustration complexes and neuroses. I find it sufficient to think of the production of distrust, moodiness, melancholy, resentment or anger – in short, of the avoidance or even destruction of an altogether necessary and desirable harmony of interpersonal relations with all their sharp corners and edges. To cut a long story short, I want to show not only the strains on the people involved in the process of education within the family, but also the need for methods of *relief*, even if these may only offer a temporary resolution of the critical situations which are inevitable in that process.

Of such necessary methods there are plenty. Their use, however, is not supported by rules, regulations or prohibitions. It is true that the enterprising discipline of pedagogy, which primarily trains teachers of all kinds, occasionally turns to education within the family circle, developing and giving well-meaning advice on relations between fathers and sons or mothers and daughters. However, it is inevitably confronted by the different degrees of intimacy in the multitude of families and the different attitudes of the persons concerned. I myself, not seeing my task as giving advice of the 'how to educate my child' type, can only follow the generally accepted end results. After all, my concern in the present context is to recognize natural impulses, regardless of whether the father or mother regards the son or daughter as a hopeless black sheep or as a praiseworthy display showpiece. The 'natural impulses' – as I call them in a deliberate attempt to avoid the depths of erudition in order to remain close to everyday life – are subject to two guiding principles, which meet in the final analysis.

One of the principles guiding the educational techniques arising from natural impulses is conditioned by the prevailing trends in society. It is in these trends that the contrast between a 'strict' and a 'lenient' education is rooted. The notion of a commonsensical introduction to social life – briefly, what must be regarded as useful, conformist, maladjusted or divergent – is determined, both as a whole and in detail, by society.

The other guiding principle results from the personality structure of the father or mother, depending on which of them sets the tone in the education process. This too is determined by the socio-cultural environment in which the persons concerned have grown up, that is, by selective factors such as family background, occupation, income and, naturally, education. While the material and non-material characteristics of one personality may have been determined by an environment in which the emphasis was placed on tough competition, in the case of another the emphasis may have been on cooperation.

How and where the two briefly outlined guiding principles – the societal and the individual – meet and merge determines the approaches chosen in critical situations within the educational process, in which, rightly or wrongly, for a variety of reasons the older people always dominate the younger. This predominance, which hangs over the entire educational process like a cloud, is the motive force of the proceedings, be it towards the desirable or undesirable, success or failure. As in a sequence of cause and effect, strict and lenient methods face each other at the extreme ends: threats ending in violence, and gentle persuasion. Threats can range from reproaches such as 'what will become of you' or 'what will people think of you', through the cane and the slap in the face, to downright maltreatment. Persuasion – in the sense of 'do it for me' or 'you'll ruin your life' etc. – employs an appeal to family sense in conjunction with friendliness, flirtatiousness and innocence as an educational method.

Both approaches oppose the independence and self-discovery which is developing – and indeed desired – in the young person, but they are managed differently according to each educator and pupil. While aggressive threats made in imperious fashion can only result in contempt or in disobedience which in its turn can reach the level of aggression, persuasion – being one of the unobtrusive variants of the art of arse-licking – is able, at least, to soothe everyday conflicts. For the rest, parents do themselves less harm, if any, by arse-licking in the form of flattery, trickery or any other expression of attention, than by trying to talk sense into their children whip in hand. It is pointless to accuse oneself of having given in too much and made too many concessions to one's children, because we are not talking about deviations but about the norm.

Parents, it is said, should set their children an example. Hence the provocative comment about people having received a good or bad education in childhood. Assuming – although it cannot be proved by the universally popular expedient of statistics – that this exemplary approach includes elements of arse-licking, arse-licking itself is likely to be imprinted on young people as one among many patterns of behaviour. To put it quite simply: no child or adolescent is stupid enough not to notice and willingly submit to arse-licking on the one hand, and not to copy and exploit it occasionally on the other – all the while seeing through this or that rule of behaviour or maxim for living, and admiring or detesting its arse-licking quality.

I read in the paper that many primary schools in Norway have introduced a new subject called 'politeness'. Pupils are expected to learn 'social behaviour' or 'rules of social intercourse'. It is reported that special emphasis is placed on teaching how to salute people by shaking hands, because this shows 'mutual respect and concern'. 'Politeness' as a subject probably includes other social graces, old-fashioned or fashionable, such as the doffing of hats or the kissing of cheeks for greeting, the ban on smacking the lips or belching when eating, and other superficial gestures of that kind. Of course these are gestures, and nothing but gestures, which moreover are employed and assessed very differently in different countries and cultures. For example, in Australia, a thoroughly western country, it is almost shocking to try to shake hands when arriving or taking leave, while the Chinese express satisfaction with a meal by audible burps.

Where education for politeness is on the agenda – in the first place presumably in the home and, should the home fail, at school – one must forget about concepts which are somewhat remote from politeness, such as etiquette, gallantry or distinction. For if the full force of politeness is recognized it counts for more than mere manners resulting from a good education and a proper sense of appropriateness. In saying 'please' and 'excuse me', one is behaving as if showing respect; in saying 'thank you', one is behaving as if showing recognition. By pretending to the extent of arse-licking one all too often creates only the *appearance* of respect or recognition for the other person, who may not necessarily deserve it. The politeness of young people being educated, and later of adults, is not always inspired, as we are told, by helpfulness, fairness, gratitude or a willingness to oblige: it only highlights externals and not what could or should be within. Aristotle already explained in the *Nicomachean Ethics* that moral dispositions are produced by actions which are similar to them.

Insofar as politeness can be regarded as a moral disposition, in a real interaction between people it consists in saying and doing anything that the other person will find pleasant. However, a prerequisite is that this should be clothed in dignity, appropriateness and honesty, and not guided or underpinned by falseness, hypocrisy or mendacity, in short, arse-licking. An old word of wisdom, taken from the *Deutsche Sinn-Gedichte* (German Epigrams) of the baron Friedrich von Logau (1604-55), says tersely what I am trying to get at in careful detail:

> Höflichkeit verlor den Rock, Falschheit hat ihn
> angezogen,
> Hat darinnen viel geäfft und manch Biederherz
> betrogen.

[Prose translation:

> Politeness lost its coat, falseness put it on,
> Aping many things, and deceiving many an
> honest heart.]

Politeness only seems to be, but is not, a virtue: it is an attribute acquired through education. We must ask therefore to what extent this attribute is still valid in our society, or to what extent it has been devalued or even, apparently, become obsolete. And if one or the other of these propositions proves correct we must ask why it is so, among young people as well as adults. For in this context people are only too ready to speak of a 'decline in standards of behaviour' or to state laconically that 'politeness is no longer in demand'. To substantiate their complaints they then point to the decay of symbolic everyday customs indicating rank such as precepts for dressing, signing letters or kissing hands;

or they deplore the emergence of bad habits such as rude interruptions in conversation, the growing use of excremental terms like 'shit', the condescending familiarity of young people addressing adults by the informal *du* rather than the formal *Sie*, and not least the increasingly sullen and uncivil behaviour of shop assistants.

Without adducing other, and much more drastic examples, we are left with the impression that the youthful sections of society follow a prevailing trend which can be called *loutishness*, and which has obviously also moved into parts of adult society. But let us continue, according to the title of this chapter, with the education of the young. Therefore: is it possible to speak of a 'return of the lout' and, if so, how did this happen?

I know full well that the term 'lout' has an old-fashioned and priggish ring, particularly as it usually carries connotations of puberty, which is marked by moody, defiant and rebellious behaviour. But I mean by 'lout' in a broader sense all those people who introduce into social intercourse an attitude of mind and a pattern of behaviour marked by excessive uncouthness, and who fail to show what they owe to themselves and to their fellow-humans.

According to the present level of research, we may well say that loutish dissensions crop up, and originate, in the years of puberty. However, as the beginning and end of puberty do not occur at the same time in all human beings loutishness in young people cannot be dismissed or condemned as a phenomenon of 'late puberty' in a way that almost amounts to an excuse. Hence parents generally try to ensure, by means of prohibitions and commands, that they do not let loose louts into adult life. If only for the sake of their own comfort – not to mention duty – they drill into boys and girls obedience and respect, including politeness as a sign of sociability, propriety, decency, considerateness and deference.

Let us now investigate whether, and how, arse-licking as a purposeful method of education plays its part in drilling respect and politeness into the young. In order to make adolescents perform one act or another – including a show of politeness – parents will give instructions. For example: 'Uncle Toby is coming. Shake hands and give him a kiss.' – 'But I don't like him. He has a revolting beard, and he smells of garlic.' – 'Do it for my sake. You know he is Daddy's boss.'

Whether unusual civility is to be applied to Uncle Toby, Aunt Melanie, or a new business partner who needs to be ensnared, the 'good manners', as they are simply labelled, contain the basic elements of arse-licking in the sense of servility, or to put it more accurately, humiliation. Observing, or merely sensing, that the parents are humiliating themselves by their polite arse-licking impairs the children's idea of the parents' obvious, in fact natural, position of power, and the result is a loss of respect.

Let us next ask what happens to the character development of young people and their preparation for life if they are themselves forced to practise arse-licking in order to be polite. Are young people steady and confident enough not to feel humiliated by this? However much the older generation may dislike it, young people, too, develop and possess a self-respect of their own, and humiliation inevitably provokes a reaction that I shall call *self-assertion*.

One conceivable way in which young people could overcome the discord between humiliation and self-assertion would be to respond to the humiliation of arse-licking by a similar behaviour. However, as they would not themselves have 'invented' the art of ensnaring, but would only be observing and imitating it, they cannot assert themselves in this way. Rather than acquiring self-respect, they would be tarnishing themselves.

It is a privilege of young people to be natural and unaffected, neither timid nor forward. But if, as happens only too often, they are deceived for educational or selfish reasons – and that by arse-licking, to boot – why should the composure demanded of them not degenerate into insolence? After all, even among adults rudeness is often sufficient to avoid being cheated by a smart-alec. Whatever we may regard as a form of loutishness – cheekiness, impudence, coarseness, naughtiness, tactlessness or impoliteness – is the product of an adolescent's recurrent reaction continuing into adulthood, for which Goethe in his play *Torquato Tasso* provided the motto 'whatever pleases is allowed'.

It is necessary to create a more or less firm balance between a conscious or unconscious insecurity in relation to the ideals of the family and society, and the ideals of the individual. This cannot be regarded as an automatic process. On the contrary. Being duped not only in a tiresome but also in a humiliating manner sets in motion complicated and positively dramatic changes in the youthful consciousness. New kinds of perception and feeling come into being, including loutishness, which are then defended rigidly and persistently. When I observe young or adult louts in everyday life, I perceive loutishness not only in their language and choice of words, but also in their manners, in their walk, in all their habits. Continuing the self-assertion they practised in response to humiliation through arse-licking in their youth, they respect nothing and believe only in themselves and in their own youth.

It would be foolhardy to pretend sourly that the 'return of the lout' in conjunction with arse-licking is a ubiquitous social trend – just as foolhardy as subscribing to the saying that 'once your reputation's done, you can blithely live for fun'. But could it not be that the individual self-realization leading to stabilization, identity or demarcation, which is granted as a right to the young, is at least imperceptibly *encouraged* by certain societal trends arising from the so-called spirit of the age? I believe that this question should not be ignored. For to say that 'the youth of today is much better than its reputation' is nothing more than a not very ingenious cliché designed to cover up one's own failure by arse-licking.

Nevertheless, we must show understanding for such a cliché, for it underlines the *cult of youth*, which in our society has been gathering ever more strength and by now verges on a trend. Starting from the Biblical injunction 'Go forth and multiply', and connected with the idea – which has for centuries maintained society – that 'the young are our future', a protective wall has been erected around young people. This follows on the one hand from the anxious premise that the young are at risk, and on the other hand from the threat to their and our own future as adults.

It is certainly a terrifying vision. And therefore, quite rightly, concerted efforts are being made to cater for the young – by the various youth authorities of the state; the religious, charitable and educational movements and institutions of the church; and both altruistic and self-serving youth associations and clubs, including the organizers of world youth festivals complete with drums and trumpets. At the same time the psychological, pedagogical, sociological or psychotherapeutical branches of 'youth research' pounce on the members of the growing generation, encircling them with questions about their preferences, role models and anxieties, about the people to whom they relate, the scenes to which they belong, and the views that they hold of their future. All this is necessary. But if we now bring the various activities which I have briefly outlined under a common denominator, we must not create a cult and give the impression that by taking an interest in the young we are sucking up to them, not say worshipping them. This is not the case if, instead of helping them, we fight emotional states peculiar to the young – selfishness, unfriendliness, intolerance and even rebelliousness – by means of prohibitions, restrictions, punishments and compulsions. It is even better to resort skilfully, that is, without deception and falsehood, to the purposive ideology of arse-licking.

Perhaps this kind of arse-licking has already been happening for a long time and is hardly condemned as immoral and reprehensible, because its indispensability is not demonstrated by obvious individual actions but rather is shimmering in the background, in the overall social context. Whether we call this background 'social context', 'collective consciousness', 'social system' or simply 'society' is irrelevant to our purpose. But it would be an unjustifiable mistake to ignore it. For whatever applies to the young under discussion is extremely closely connected to the social context, which in its turn is subject to a comprehensive 'social' or 'societal change' unfolding slowly at some times and fast at others.

Ever since its beginnings, sociology has observed and analysed the problem of social change in order to recognize and supply grounds for social judgments. It has done so by identifying *trends* running through society, while constantly underlining that the identification of trends is an impersonal operation, and using the term, as should be obvious, without any ineluctable moral implications. Without going too far back in time, we once spoke of the trend of 'marketing orientation', later of 'other-directedness', then again of 'identity dispersal' and of the 'age of incoherence'. At the moment the social firmament is illuminated by the trend paraphrased in the slogan of the 'permissive society', which may soon be overshadowed by a counter-trend made up of 'political correctness' and 'virtuality'. It should be borne in mind that none of these descriptions endows the trend concerned with the quality of a permanent norm. Nevertheless, all of them – including the phrase 'permissive society' – are substantial indications of what society, or certain social groups, including the young, desire and expect at the present time.

Within the scope of this study I do not propose to examine the trend towards the permissive society or to provide proofs of its existence, particulary as I have no intention of either denouncing or defending it. We are simply faced with a product of social conditions which is changing as rapidly as the social conditions themselves. For the rest, I will stay with young people, here as in the whole of this chapter. At this point I will demonstrate, in exemplary fashion and with reference to some customs and moral norms relating to sexuality and sexual morality, how society supports the young – that is, the *audacity* that they owe to their biological development – by means of the social trend of

permissiveness, indulgence, forebearance and tolerance, in a word, by arse-licking.

As an observable example from the life of the
young I will take music and dancing, which can
never be understood apart from the rest of the society
concerned. The kind of dance peculiar to today's
youth has replaced the 'closed dance', in which the
partners touch each other, with the 'partnerless
dance', so to speak a solo dance without physical contact. It all takes place accompanied by a music produced at a stupendous volume, which envelops the
dancers, creating a quasi-euphoria and making conversation as good as impossible. This phenomenon,
together with others of a similar nature, is characteristic of the attitude of a young generation to which
the taboos based on earlier norms are no longer
applicable. It is indeed the expression of a permissive
society, which, instead of exercising the taboos concerning contact with the other sex and suppressing
rebellion, looks the other way, allowing the young to
behave according to their own conventions, that is, to
be sexually alert, relatively uninhibited and at the
same time self-assured.

To provide another example of a life style which
would not be possible without arse-licking, I may note
that boys and girls nowadays chat open-heartedly
about masturbation, defloration, the pill, homosexual-
ity, group sex or prostitution, not to mention the fact
that they are shown love, lust, sex and passion in their
most naked form even by such purportedly reputable

media as public television. In other words, a permissive society has made it possible for moral norms and moral actions to reveal aspects which no longer correspond to traditional moral conventions. Here too a permissive society as it were licks the arse of youth, just as it does in taboo-breaking films, musicals, plays, records or printed publications. And this not for 'entertainment', as it would be for adults, but as a first step into a larger world than that of a rural village or a provincial slum. Hence the hopelessness of any prohibitions, by whatever authority, including parents, that may pronounce and try to enforce them.

It is as erroneous to maintain that the permissive society recognizes only the criterion of social harmfulness, as it is inadequate to believe that a permissive society, operating by arse-licking, implies the presence of an intelligent young generation, rather than a stupid one in need of protection. Otherwise the current calls for knowledge would not be so vociferous. It is necessary to understand that this desire ranges from the intellectual to the physical, from the moral to the immoral, from the tabloid to the quality paper, from informative non-fiction books to sex magazines, video clips and data banks.

Let us beware of regarding the use of arse-licking, from whichever side of the education process that I have demonstrated, simply as a vice. As a purposive ideology, it has a social function in everyday life, unless it is stretched to such a degree as to prove a system of maintaining and controlling power. In that event we would lose our respect for one another, and indeed our respect for life as our supreme possession.

XII

Adaptation
Avoidance of conflict, voluntary and enforced

A. Paul Weber: Saved (1966)

I had long hesitated to connect 'adaptation' with the art of arse-licking. After all, adapting to a person, an object or a situation is basically a normal, not to say innocent, process: one accepts reality and submits to it. However, when adaptation follows crooked paths, when it stoops to soft-soaping, it forfeits good faith, abandons principles and loses its worth. Let us think only of two leading lights in our cultural life – the writer Gerhart Hauptmann and the composer Richard Strauss – and the speed with which they paid their most abject respects to the Hitler regime. Adaptation therefore is not so simple as to allow us to say that it consists of any given kind of adjustment. Otherwise we would not praise, admire or despise those who know how to use all possible methods of adaptation, in word and deed, to further their own aims.

In the foreground is the search for success – prestige, profit, social standing, popularity, or integration into a group, organization or whole section of society. To put it more mundanely, adaptation is directed, with or without arse-licking, at getting one's way without giving offence or suffering injury. However, this does not answer the question about the intrinsic object of adaptation, that is, about just what is being adapted when one adapts oneself. The answer can only be: one's way of comporting oneself, one's *behaviour*. In saying this, I diverge from the biological model of 'adaptation to the environment', and I regard the actions involved in adaptation as modes of behaviour. Adaptation, together with arse-licking as a method, is largely a mode of behaviour which has become a habit. Whether, and to what extent, adaptation permeates one's whole way of life depends – as does arse-licking – on the impulses of the individual and on the operation of this pre-formed behavioural pattern.

As a preparation for the topic of 'adaptation' as one of the manifestations of arse-licking one could make many sociological points. For instance, one could talk about non-adaptation and its relationship to cultural lag, or one could examine the question whether it is not only the people who adapt to the system, but also the system that adapts to the people. But at the risk of disappointing some expectations – if indeed it is a disappointment – I must refrain from proceeding in the manner of a textbook, or else I could miss the wood for the trees and confound the reader's own 'behaviour'.

Let us experience the joy of discovery by looking adaptation – that state of inconsistency and disparity between ends and means – squarely in the eye, bearing in mind that it is blinded, more or less, by arse-licking. In so doing, I shall, as always, keep to every-day life, whether its light falls on the individual or on a collective. It is not given to anybody, including me, to follow up all the innumerable processes of adaptation. Consequently I can only select a few processes which, even if they do not appear typical in all fundamental respects, will reveal their importance in connection with the art of arse-licking.

I could take the easy way out by choosing banalities from the lowest level of adaptation, culminating in trite words of wisdom like 'always say something instructive or binding', 'never talk about anything that wouldn't interest anyone but you' or 'don't ridicule the weakest members of society', and in calls like 'keep talking' or 'make it short'. We must set our sights higher, and there we find – still with everyday occurrences in mind – the eventful relationships and communications between men and women. In an ideal partnership each partner is expected to feel and think exactly like the other. But this would be downright 'inhuman' and unrealistic. It would preclude any exchange of opinions, any stimulating debate, and thus any argument and conflict: communication would collapse into itself, into deadly boredom, into unbounded autism. This 'downfall' must be prevented, if only for the sake of self-preservation. In other words, as conflicts develop a dynamic of their own, their solution, or at least their alleviation, also develops its own dynamic. One of the proven methods of achieving this is arse-licking.

In the first place I perceive a silent body language which consists of looks and gestures corresponding to natural feelings. Whether this body language involves a wistful or childishly playful glance or a humbly inclined head, its aim is to create peace, even if this is done with hypocritical reservations. In the heat of the argument the looks and gestures may be received as sincere or feigned ones, but the element of arse-licking contained in them is close to submission, to a display of obsequiousness.

Of greater importance for the alleviation of conflicts between men and women is linguistic adaptation. Since quarrels are usually accompanied by – or rooted in – reproaches, those familiar with the art of arse-licking will think carefully about the opening sentence of a discussion in order to avoid flaunting their superiority. They will throw in a compliment or even a joke, so as not to arouse any possible suspicion of condescension by using a phrase like 'oh, stop it' or 'I don't want to hear that'. For just as not listening runs counter to all the rules of arse-licking, expressing needs – most commonly concerning the clarification of a misunderstanding – in an amorphous language is a humiliatingly obvious form of it. Things that occur in the heat of the moment are uncontrollable, and I will disregard them, just as I will disregard the ignorant waffle about counselling, a platitude which always asks for trouble.

A subject about which people do not like to talk in this context is sex and sexuality, although its cover of intimacy has long since fallen away. What was once demonstrated to us by means of the sex lives of ants is today performed in every other film or television programme, lying or standing up, wildly or gently, roughly or tenderly. And what once was only done, but not talked about, today fills whole pages of popular magazines aimed at young people or adults. This is a good thing, for it illustrates the defeat of prudish prejudices, puritanical convictions and a notion of sinfulness stoked by the churches and self-appointed moralists. The blindness and secrecy hovering over the sex act have disappeared, not least thanks to the scientific study of human sexuality. 'Sex research', as it is called, operates on a large scale and without reservations, extending its investigations in all imaginable directions: the relationship between society and culture and the forms taken by sexuality in different social and cultural environments; the establishment of sexual identities; the dynamic of sexual urges; the social construction of sexual dangers; the interaction between sexuality and health; and many more.

Without wishing to cast doubt on the necessity and value of these researches, I feel that they fail to illuminate a crucial aspect of the sexual activity of young or old, married or unmarried partners, namely the significance of sex in holding together or in separating couples. Precisely because sexuality is not only an instinct or a mere biological need, but a serious emotional relationship between human beings, it has – as a mystery created by God – powers which transcend the purely physical. I feel justified in saying that it is pointless, and alien to everyday reality, to deny sanctimoniously that sexuality, this special kind of 'feeling', is both an inducement and a bonding force in all its stages, from seductive billing and cooing, through falling in love, to legal or anarchic cohabitation or parting. Thus it makes use of social factors, although its dynamic varies so greatly from one case to another that its manifestations can more easily be estimated than directly observed. The only certainty is that, where cohesion is desired, in happy or unhappy circumstances, the partners must adapt to each other, be it, crudely put, in sexual *tours de force* or abstinence.

But where, in respect of adaptation to sexual entanglements, are the hiding-places of arse-licking? As I have no intention of making myself look ridiculous by presenting constructive methods or models for recording and analysing the aforesaid feelings, or by substantiating needs and emotions through external actions – e.g. reluctantly but repeatedly 'giving oneself' – I turn to the social elements which influence and determine the life of society. Here I first encounter the manifestation of a person's value. Sexual intercourse is subject to the order of nature or propagation as well as to the order of the person, that is, to love and lust. Every act, whether its aim is the production of a child or a loving or lustful advance to a partner, acknowledges the value of the person in an adaptive manner. This can happen both openly and deceitfully: the personal management of the sexual union therefore opens the doors to arse-licking, of the kind that manipulates an *emotional state*.

In the same context we may mention the ability of human beings to modify congenital instincts and, for example, to shape sexuality according to their own image of humanity. In so doing they either employ the anatomical and physiological resources received from nature or they light a fire of affection and gratitude. This rational and emotional control, genuine or feigned, adapts itself, on the one hand, to the pursuit of the physical and emotional well-being of the partner, and, on the other hand, to the preservation of one's own personality, that is, the avoidance of dependency, for which any method of arse-licking is right and proper.

We can list several other aspects of sexual adaptation with or without arse-licking. For example, the relationship between the sexes as determined by the domination of men and the opposition of the emancipatory women's movement, which – particularly where sex and sexuality are concerned – always awakens a suspicion of hypocrisy by protesting rather aggressively in public against something practised, as is human, in private. One could also talk about the necessity of emotional maturity in sexual encounters that recognize and cultivate values transcending the fake moans and grunts which are paraded in films and television programmes to simulate passion, and which therefore create the impression of arse-licking. Finally I should mention the concurrence of physical and intellectual development, which reflects an adapted emotional state, free of arse-licking.

I may say that so far my discussion of adaptation accompanied by arse-licking has been quite moderate. There is a good reason for this. I have assumed a type of adaptation, or adaptive instinct, rooted in human nature, from which it derives a power that cannot easily be resisted. I have throughout envisaged a kind of adaptation that occurs basically without coercion, voluntarily, of its own accord, albeit here and there carrying a whiff of arse-licking. To put it clearly: we have so far only dealt with one of two categories of adaptation, namely with adaptation without coercion, of which arse-licking can only be an accessory.

But what about the other category? What happens when adaptation is enforced, when adaptation must be equated with arse-licking, when whole population groups are regarded as arse-lickers? In such cases, surely, it is not possible to speak of adaptation as an innate urge for self-approval and for approval by others. Here, with arse-licking equalling adaptation and adaptation equalling arse-licking, adaptation no longer stems from the natural desire of people to be in the good books of their fellow-humans, but from a desire which is so strong and compelling that it demands the use of arse-licking in order to be satisfied.

It is hardly surprising that as a Jew I will cite as an example the group of my fellow-Jews, an ethnic minority, particularly as we have always been regarded, by well-meaning as well as ill-disposed parties, as being competent at adaptation and arse-licking – which, incidentally, is true and has contributed over the centuries to our *survival*. Without wishing to arouse philo-Semitic pity, I must note that the history of the Jews has been a history of suffering, a history moving between persecution and exodus. None of the countless partial or comprehensive studies of the history of the Jews, old or new, fails to document innumerable events, situations and circumstances marked by *suffering*: from the Babylonian exile to the fall of Jerusalem; from the schism between Judaism and Christianity, the subsequent pogroms during the Crusades and the slanderous accusations of 'ritual murder' and 'desecration of the Host', to the ejection from Spain; from the epoch of Humanism and Reformation to the emancipatory Enlightenment of the eighteenth century and to our own day – 'suffering' as a characteristic form of life constantly breaks through the pages of Jewish historiography. At the same time, one must not forget that the physical, existential or intellectual sufferings undergone by Jews were often caused by themselves, and that the history of the Jews also shows periods of well-being without suffering.

If we consider the history of the Jews in relation to the towns and villages, countries and continents in which, temporarily or permanently, they have lived or are still living, we see a picture of migrations round the globe. Whether they were caused by wars, persecutions, evictions, atrocities or other external pressures, in each case these relocations imposed a process of adaptation on the Jews. In so saying I am describing a condition which implies the uncompromising notion of *coercion*. Wherever the ethnic minority went, it was faced by a dominating and driving force to which it was obliged to submit. This submission, which included the methods of arse-licking, not only obeyed necessity but also made those engaged in the adaptation and arse-licking aware of their dependence and alleged inferiority. This is my starting point for demonstrating, by means of an example, how adaptation under coercion leads to arse-licking, almost producing an equation in which it may be society, the spirit of the age or the state, as well as certain population groups that engender the submission and humiliation.

When the Jew Heinrich Heine, Germany's unsurpassed lyric poet, was born in Düsseldorf in 1797 the majority of Jews in Germany lived in conditions of oppression and confinement, not unlike those of the Middle Ages. Although most of the ghetto walls behind which the Jews were crammed had fallen, the written and unwritten laws and regulations restricting their freedom remained in force. At the same time, the spirit of the Enlightenment and the French Revolution of 1789, and not least the Napoleonic liberations, supplied Jews with opportunities of emancipation, as it is called, and, within the process of this emancipatory movement, of assimilation, i.e. adaptation.

The legislature intervened in the development of the Jews' emancipatory and assimilatory ways of life. First, there was the so-called 'Hardenberg Jewish Edict' of 11 March 1812, which granted civic rights to Jews when the 15-year-old Heine was still at school. Second, there was the Cabinet Order of the reactionary King Frederick William III dated 18 August 1823, which cancelled many of the civic rights granted to Jews by Hardenberg's edict, when Heine was a fourth-year law student. This was a slap in the face for the efforts that had been made for decades to bring about the integration of the Jewish population into the social as well as cultural structure of the state. For the lawyer Heine, who aspired to a possible university career, it was the end of that dream, because the royal Cabinet Order stipulated, among other things, that Jews should no longer be admitted to teaching positions in Prussia.

Heine spent his childhood and youth in an atmosphere of equal rights in a clan in which belonging to the Jewish faith and emphatically practising its rituals played a much smaller part than adapting to the secular position of being Jewish, and thereby finding a firm place, secured by equal rights, in the surrounding non-Jewish world – in short, what is simply described as assimilation. Of religiousness in the sense of belief and compliance with laws and rites there was no question. These were what to this day are called 'assimilated Jews', members of the Jewish faith who, while not breaking with Judaism, absorbed as far as possible the culture, the way of life and the habits of thought prevailing in the country in which they lived.

In June 1825, barely a month before obtaining his doctorate, Harry Heine converted to Protestantism and changed his first name to Heinrich. Heine's biographers have devoted hundreds of pages to these decisive events in his life, elucidating the reasons for his conversion on the one hand, and the consequences regarding his life and thought on the other. I do not intend to summarize all this here. I can only say that Heine was not moved by religious reasons but only by the consideration of what would help him complete his partial assimilation without arse-licking. To wit: the attempt to escape the lack of rights still affecting Jews; connected with this, the intention to carry assimilation to a point where a successful career, particularly of an academic kind, would become accessible; and, not least, the desire to throw off the burden of Jewish culture in favour of German and European culture, which is documented by Heine's much-quoted statement in his *Gedanken und Einfälle* (Thoughts and Ideas): 'The certificate of baptism is the ticket of admission to European culture.'

None of it materialized. And so we see, when we contemplate the life of the converted Heine from this point of view, how his efforts to settle as an advocate in Hamburg miscarried, as did his exertions to obtain a professorship in Berlin or a chair of literature at the University of Munich. His grovelling concession to Christian society, designed to put the finishing touches to adaptation under the pseudonym of assimilation, had not only failed to reach its goal, but had earned him, as with so many other renegades, profound enmities. It was not to take him long, about one year after his conversion, to write to a friend: 'I am now hated by Christians and Jews. I very much regret converting. Nothing shows me that I have been doing better since. On the contrary, I have had nothing since but misfortune.' Indeed, the enterprise of conversion proved a failure, both for Heine personally and for his assimilatory enterprise. As always, he had to continue living in an environment loaded with anti-Jewish prejudices, in which he could not develop freely. He was driven 'hence' by the misery of the 'Jew that could not be washed off', as he wrote, and he emigrated to Paris.

The same fate as Heine's befell many other Jews who discarded their religion in favour of Christianity, as a result of conviction, adaptation, coercion or necessity. The Jew Gustav Mahler for instance, as we have seen, would never have been appointed director of the Vienna Court Opera if he had not become a Catholic beforehand. The same happened to the Cologne Jewish boy Jakob – called Jacques – Offenbach, and to many Jewish scientists and scholars, not to be listed here, whose access to an academic career remained blocked until they converted to Christianity – incidentally, a situation which continued into the third decade of our own century.

Now that we have reached the present we should

mention the many fully assimilated German, Austrian, Hungarian, Polish and Czech Jews, who chose baptism in order to escape the Nazi gangs, which, as we know, did nothing to help them. For the Nazis treated them as they did Heine, Germany's greatest lyric poet, whom they were unable to kill but managed to reduce to 'Anon' in their anthologies.

The simultaneity of enforced adaptation and necessary arse-licking, as demonstrated here by the example of a German cultural genius, affects all Jews as a result of their Jewishness. They either experience it themselves, in their own social and cultural position, or they observe it in their fellow-Jews, or they learn about it from tradition, references in prayers, religious education and, most of all, from reports about ejection, mass murders, emigration, discrimination or anti-Semitic excesses. These insights are due not to an often invoked historical consciousness, but to a collective consciousness manifesting itself as collective memory and collective conscience, which has appropriated and engraved upon itself the history of suffering as the history of the collective. Unceasingly projecting the historical past on to the present and a hopeful future, this consciousness constantly affects the Jew's being. It is imprinted on the determinants of a common destiny to which the individual remains attached, even if he has never had to suffer with it, if he has cut himself off from it, or if he denies or indeed fights it as an agnostic or renegade. Just as each Jew carries the history of suffering on his shoulders, so

Adaptation

does the spirit of proving his worth by survival mark the concrete reality of each Jew. Let no-one blame him for practising adaptation through the art of arse-licking.

XIII

Guilt-Shedding
Of perpetrators and victims

Carl Spitzweg: Customs officer in action (*c*. 1860)

Guilt-Shedding

✍

In my passage through the manifestations of arse-licking I have more than once encountered the concept of 'corruption' as a reprehensible activity. I did not attribute much significance to this in relation to my own topic: after all, am I really engaged in arse-licking – or doing anything wrong – if I slip the head waiter in a restaurant a tip to secure a comfortable table for myself and my guests? Doing a favour, without the humiliation or coercion involved in arse-licking, could at worst be described as bribery. But is that also the case when bribery, the hallmark of corruption, reaches a disturbing degree in political, economic and social life? Is arse-licking still not in play, or does it contribute to the proceedings? In other words, should I include corruption – whether it presents itself in the form of bribery, official patronage, taking advantage, granting privileges, or offering inducements – in my manual of everyday arse-licking, and should I support the prophets of moral doom by regarding arse-licking, as soon as it appears, as corruption and even a punishable offence?

I can hear people ask why I worry about such

subtleties when I read, day in, day out, about corruption concerning handouts to officials and the quagmire of political favours, the impact of corruption on the administration, the police and the judiciary, and, not least, corruption in the shape of economic crimes – tax evasion, rackets involving subsidies, insurance and bankruptcy, trade in arms and human beings, the usurious deals of slum landlords, embezzlement and fraud.

Those who ask such a question, that is, those who from the start regard corruption – whether by words or money, favouritism, intrigue or manipulation, temptation, pressure or incitement – as a criminal offence, overlook not only its semantic breadth but also its implications of moral degeneracy and decay. Imagine what it means if corruption today is said to be part of the system in any given country. Does not this notion endow the spirit of corruption with an importance far beyond arse-licking? It does so insofar as in everyday parlance the imputation of corruption always has a profoundly unsettling effect on large organizations, such as a state, a party or a big business enterprise, while calling individuals corrupt or corruptible only attaches a potentially punishable blemish to them.

A tricky situation arises if one tries to free corruption from the stigma of arse-licking, and arse-licking from the stigma of corruption. Perhaps this is due to an overly narrow or overly broad definition and application of the term, as if it were a maid of all work. To obtain pertinent information, we would really need to consult a 'History of Corruption', but I looked in vain for such a work. What I myself have managed to produce in this line is also pretty thin, but I will briefly report it to demonstrate that I cannot be put off my guilt-shedding enterprise by gloomy judgements.

In *Arthasastra*, a book on political and economic relations by the semi-mythical Indian statesman Kautilya (300 BC), I have read that there are no government servants who do not take money for themselves or consume part of the king's income. When ancient Greece said farewell to the city-state in the fifth century or so, corruption there is also supposed to have reached fairly serious proportions. To continue concisely: historical research informs us of how victories, booty, ostentation and wealth brought corruption on a broad front to the administration of the Roman Empire. In the Holy Roman Empire, owing to the constant search for profits and to social and economic inequalities, corruption in the state and the church was so widespread that the philosopher and statesman Francis Bacon called it one of the four vices of power. And as parliament in the course of the centuries attained an increasingly important position bribery and corruption virtually became an organized feature of parliamentary elections.

These few historical hints are only meant to indicate that corruption is nothing new, and that, with a small adjustment to the spirit of our time and society, we can show it to be the same as ever. Nevertheless, it would be unrealistic to measure the motives of the whole complex of corruption in the past with the same yardstick as those of the present, and it would be foolhardy to place them on a par with arse-licking. Unlike arse-licking, every case of corruption is a dramatic construct – in particular as far as the structure of the motives is concerned – and consists of the following:

- an *action*: that which takes place in thought and deed;
- a *scene*: the background to the action, or the situation in which the action occurs;
- one or more *actors*: the person, or kind of person, who carries out the action;
- the *methods*: the ways and means which are employed;
- and finally the *purpose*: what is to be achieved.

Seen as a whole, the motivation of any given case of corruption is revealed by the relationship between scene and action, scene and actors, scene and methods, and scene and purpose. Social actions are used, to entice an individual, to divert political, economic or legal bodies from performing their duties, to undermine the well-being of the community, and so on. It is a fundamental aspect of corruption as a social activity that it destroys everything that is considered honest, orderly, regular and intact in the communal life of human beings, regardless of how honesty, innocence, soundness and even sanctity are devastated in the process. Corruption is motivated by depravity, breeding disruption, distortion and dehumanization – which is sufficient reason for defying it and making it punishable.

I admit that in drawing the necessary line between corruption and arse-licking I succumbed to a passion which ill befits the sobriety of a sociologist. But it was important to avoid confusing the relatively easily recognizable breach of existing norms – in the case of corruption, for instance, the offer and acceptance of bribes or the abuse of a public office – with one form or other of arse-licking, which may at first sight be perceived as an essentially impenetrable art.

At this point the question arises how I can be so bold as to associate arse-licking with our sublime concept of art, rather than calling it, in a more restrained and restrictive manner, a *skill*. This would be fully justified if I had not regarded arse-licking, right from the beginning of my manual, more or less as a game of hide-and-seek, played adroitly at some times and clumsily at others, which should be neither justified nor condemned and which, to put it briefly, is absorbed in the superficiality of everyday life. To achieve such a threadbare aim, it is enough to make a list of the *perceptible* breaches of social norms, customs and morality committed by the arse-licker.

Such a manual of the art of arse-licking would contain, among others, the following guidelines:

- Season your arse-licking conversations with innuendos and ambiguities.

- Arouse the curiosity of the person you want to soft-soap by oblique questions, without making the mood heavy.
- Confuse your interlocutor by unpleasant, unsettling, but also cheerful and amusing news.
- Never get to the point at once and never be concise, but make the topic interesting by long-windedness.
- Affect openness to prevent the impression that you are covering up weaknesses and fear.
- Allow your victims to show themselves to their greatest advantage.
- Insist that, rather than wishing to hurt anybody, you are putting yourself in their place.
- Whether you are giving a show of discretion, applause, easy manners, fidelity or kindness, always remember that your intention is to use people for your own ends and to mobilise everybody at will for your selfish schemes.

Arse-licking, as demonstrated by these few examples, follows the principle of utility, but is marked by a conspicuously crude simplicity. In order to rise above mere intuition, to the level of art in the sense of a skill, refinement is needed, here as in all forms of everyday life. 'Refinement' leading to artistic perfection generally begins with a learning phase, followed by practice and repetition, till it achieves the autonomy and responsibility that we commonly call *mastery*. It is only at this point that arse-licking can be applied in a strategically astute and meaningful manner, holding its ground in difficult situations, succeeding even in unfavourable circumstances, and becoming potentially pernicious. However, the art of arse-licking cannot be acquired by any established process of learning, let alone practice, but at best by imitation. Where then should we look for our starting position in the process of guilt-shedding in respect of its justification or lack of justification? Despite all our reservations it will perhaps be helpful to resort to intuition, that is, to an emotional and instinctive understanding.

It is claimed that the internal nature of reality is not recognized by reason but by intuition. This, however, cannot satisfy an empiricist exploring the reality of arse-licking. For intuition, instead of allowing us to discover how things are in themselves, divides reality, both static and in motion, into incoherent and immovable fragments, which can in no way facilitate or promote arse-licking within the framework of real, or practical, reason. We have not yet found an alternative for the fact that reason pervades both the simple and the complex activities of thinking, and that all understanding is the work of reason. Conversely, the incoherent elements of intuition, on whose shoulders arse-licking all too often falls, cannot lead to true understanding.

It is sometimes assumed that knowing how to play on the weaknesses of human beings enables one to turn them into anything one wants by means of the simple-minded acts of arse-licking listed above. But the people who make this assumption become unavoidably embroiled in a struggle between rationalism and irrationalism, losing sight of those aspects of *moral reality* which, whether we like it or not, guide us in all our actions, including arse-licking. Oh dear, I hear you say, why venture into the area of morality when it is enough to show that where practical reason is absent all appeals to it are pointless. I would indeed be on the wrong track if I were to start moralizing. For debates about misdemeanours in the context of arse-licking do not bring us an inch further: they would only be a kind of surrogate action distracting us from the real subject. However, the researcher into matters of everyday life should not – as is mostly the case – recoil from demarcating moral positions. After all, is there anything more important about morality than its application to life?

Arse-licking, in whatever form, confronts its user with two manifestations of moral reality: the objective and the subjective. The objective manifestation consists of an accumulation of maxims and behavioural precepts developed by society. As moral rules, these maxims and precepts prescribe how one must behave towards one's fellow-humans. If they are infringed, as in the case of arse-licking, it is not the specific inner nature of the action that entails a sanction or punishment, but, if anything at all, the fact that the action does not agree with the rules which society considers binding. As a subjective manifestation of moral reality, arse-licking aims directly at the quasi-'sacred' personality of a human being. By penetrating its enclosure, arse-licking violates this personality, as it does goodness as such.

Whether arse-licking is guided by perseverance, enthusiasm, responsibility, kindness, expediency or even heroism, its real morality is controlled by those elements of 'human nature' which serve the harmonious satisfaction of both individual and social desires. The hinterland of arse-licking as a purposive ideology is provided by aspects of moral reality founded on practical reason. These liberate the individual from the fetters of the moral and social conventions that confine, constrict, and sometimes reduce him to insignificance. If one has perfectly mastered the art of arse-licking one will always know how to combine objective and subjective moral reality in one's demands, if only to discover oneself or, to put it arrogantly, 'to be what one is'.

This 'being', which is only rarely confronted and analysed because of its disreputable quality, needs encouragement. For, although arse-licking is not listed as a punishable offence, it is nevertheless marked by guilt. From whatever angle we have studied arse-licking behaviour – the complaisant solicitude for the actions of one's fellow-humans – we have always found defects such as exploitation, coercion, humiliation, aversion, servility, self-interest, atonement or ridicule. Where arse-licking appears in its full glory and artistry, time passes and pain is left behind.

In this process the victim is not taken into consideration: on the contrary, free rein is given to the satisfaction of wishes and desires according to the principle of living at the expense of others. We are facing a mundane, surprisingly overt process of interaction, motivated by what is generally described as need. For we know that the behaviour of the individual is influenced by needs, albeit always in conjunction with rampant desires as well as ideas, models and values. To connect the motivation of the need for arse-licking with milieu, situation, or stimulus-and-reaction sequences seems wrong to me. For this would bring arse-licking close to a necessity, a requirement of social life, alienating it and depriving it of its most prominent attribute: *voluntariness*.

With the exception of the kind of social pressure that I demonstrated, in the chapter on adaptation, through the example of the Jewish ethnic minority, nobody is nudged or forced by external factors into arse-licking. The arse-licker acts freely, loves arse-licking, and thus proves 'worthy' of it. Regardless of any benefit that he may achieve or any harm that he may inflict, and regardless of any incriminating faults, vice or immorality, he freely establishes for himself a value, which he measures according to what he admires and what he considers worthless, and which represents his *self-esteem*. This self-esteem, transcending material values and enabling the arse-licker to shed the guilt of unjustified, immoral or even criminal behaviour, comprises the belief which asserts that 'I am better than the other fellow.'

From here it is not a long way to *self-love*. Arse-licking, handled so skilfully as to resemble a favour, betokens the paradox of being at one and the same time the perpetrator and the victim. Aroused, on the one hand, by the desire never to be deceived, but not wishing, on the other hand, to refuse the chance of receiving flattery, self-love is supported intellectually and emotionally by an aversion to the truth that can rise to the degree of hatred. In this predicament, the arse-licker feels impelled in his behaviour to destroy the truth, hiding his faults – or his imperfection – both from himself and from the other person. It is undoubtedly an evil to have faults, Pascal says in his *Pensées*, but it is an even greater evil to have them and not want to know them, since this means deliberately adding deception to them.

Without putting too much distance between living reality and the process of guilt-shedding by forsaking the love of truth, we must note that the arse-licker sometimes finds himself in a position of having to tolerate what he neither wants, nor loves, nor respects. And as this has already been demonstrated in the course of our various investigations, we may say, without going into further explanations, that lack of respect is not always an offence, and manifestations of hatred may sometimes be close to virtues. Certainly, disapproval, impatience, cantankerousness – in short, intolerance – is an accessory of arse-licking, but does not the admissible, and tolerable, also carry some elements of the contemptible and detestable? Let us face it: tolerance is part of the human heritage.

What I have claimed here does not exonerate arse-licking but enables it to shed its accumulated guilt by falling back on itself, that is, by its entanglement in the dilemma of being at one and the same time a perpetrator who sets the standards and a victim. It is easy to say that people would not live long in society if they were not all both tricksters and dupes, but when survival is at stake – that is, when the question arises whether or not arse-licking can be justified not to others, but to oneself – self-justification gains the upper hand.

It is no great piece of wisdom to declare that in this world human beings only count for what they make of themselves, but it is an art to be an arse-licker and to know how to hide it.

Index